Lucian Freud: recent work

WHITECHAPEL

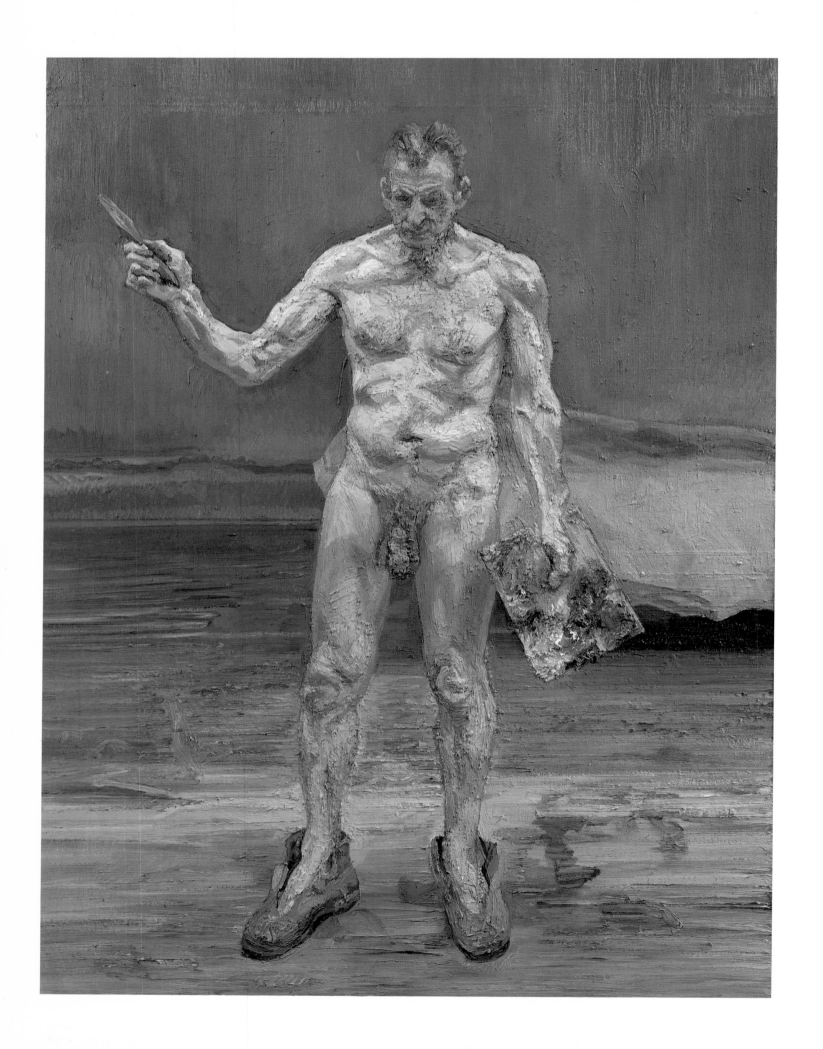

Whitechapel Art Gallery, London
The Metropolitan Museum of Art, New York
Museo Nacional Centro de Arte Reina Sofía, Madrid

Catherine Lampert

Lucian Freud:recent work

Whitechapel Art Gallery, London
10 September – 21 November 1993

The Metropolitan Museum of Art, New York
16 December 1993 – 13 March 1994

Museo Nacional Centro de Arte Reina Sofía, Madrid
19 April – 21 June 1994

An exhibition organised by the Whitechapel Art Gallery,
80–82 Whitechapel High Street, London E1

In association with

This catalogue has received support from
Global Asset Management Limited

ISBN 0–8548–8103–4

Cover: Double Portrait, 1985–86
Oil on canvas, 31 × 35 ins/78.75 × 89 cm
Private Collection

Contents

Foreword

The Whitechapel Art Gallery was extremely pleased when four years ago Lucian Freud agreed to show his new paintings and etchings in 1993. The prospect has become ever more enticing as ambitious and beautiful works have been completed and more and more they become a group that should be seen at least once altogether. It is also gratifying that this exhibition will be shared with The Metropolitan Museum of Art and the Museo Nacional Centro de Arte Reina Sofía since the American and Spanish public have had few opportunities to see Freud's work. In this respect the team organising the London show who included my colleagues, Felicity Lunn and Rebecca Hurst (and virtually everyone else in the Gallery), have greatly benefited from the involvement of William S. Lieberman, Jacques and Natasha Gelman Chairman of 20th Century Art at the Metropolitan, whose familiarity with Freud's work dates from the 1940s, and Anne L. Strauss, Research Associate in the Department of 20th Century Art, Philippe de Montebello, Director and Mahrukh Tarapor, Associate Director for Exhibitions at the Metropolitan. We are also grateful for the assistance and support given by Maria de Corral, the Director of the Museo Nacional Centro de Arte Reina Sofía and others there, especially Marta Gonzalez. The added section of important paintings from the years prior to 1982 for the showings abroad has made further demands on the owners. Deprived of their works for ten months, all the lenders deserve our thanks.

Very direct practical help in organising this exhibition has been given to the Whitechapel by Frank Auerbach, during the selection; by the artist's former and present dealers, James Kirkman, William Acquavella, Duncan MacGuigan, Matthew Marks and Brooke Alexander; by Derek Birdsall, Martin Lee and their colleagues at Omnific who designed and produced the catalogue, printed in Milan by Pizzi; by Baroness Willoughby d'Eresby; by Momart and the other transport agents; by Rizzoli who will distribute the catalogue outside Europe; and by the Museums and Galleries Commission who have arranged U.K. Government Indemnity. Furthermore, the U.S. Government Federal Council on the Arts and the Humanities has awarded to The Metropolitan Museum of Art an indemnity for the project.

In spite of Freud's reputation, it has not been easy to find corporate support for
the exhibition and therefore the organisers are more than usually indebted to
those who have made contributions: to The Observer, and Liz Bolton and Mike
Feld at Pragmatism who arranged this association of the newspaper with the
London exhibition, and to Global Asset Management Limited, the Horace
W. Goldsmith Foundation and The British Council. Over the past year the
following people and organisations (and others not mentioned) have helped in
various and generous ways: Bruce Bernard, Monique Beudert, Jenny Blyth, Paul
Bonaventura, Gilbert de Botton, Brian Boylan, Susie Boyt, Richard Calvocoressi,
Melanie Clore, Sharon H. Cott, Magdalena Dabrowski, James Demetrion,
Andrew Dempsey, Maureen Duggan, William Feaver, Jacqueline Ford, Lee
White Galvis, Thomas Gibson, Robert Gordon, Anthony Grant, Jasper Johns,
Hal and Jesse Kant, The Ruth and Stuart Lipton Charitable Trust, Thomas
Llorens, Irene Martin, Steve Martin, Susana Martinez-Garrido, Therese Meier,
Charles Miers, Robert Miller, Lucy Mitchell-Innes, Herbert M. Moskowitz,
David J. Nash, Simon de Pury, Emily K. Rafferty, Cora Rosavear, Andrea Rose,
Charles Saatchi, Nicholas Serota, Mercedes Stoutzker, Linda M. Sylling, Julian
Treuherz, Valerie Troyansky, and Francis Wynham.

I joined the Arts Council shortly before it organised Lucian Freud's first
retrospective at the Hayward Gallery in 1974 and from that time I became
especially attached to the work. Since 1982 I have been visiting the studio, not
least during preparations for his second Hayward show in 1988, and have been
spoiled by the surprise and by seeing the compelling look of the works on the
easel, in progress and then finished but unframed. Lucian Freud has a very
strong idea of how the pictures should be seen together and it is the
Whitechapel's privilege that he will help install the show in London. Indeed,
he has contributed in every way to making the exhibition and the publication,
and has gone further by offering works completed since June 1993.

Catherine Lampert
Director, Whitechapel Art Gallery

Lucian Freud : recent work

Catherine Lampert

Lucian Freud

And the Bridegroom 1991–92, one of the largest works Lucian Freud has ever painted, answers one ambition he defined in 1954. Insisting on the priority of the painter's undiluted taste, he explained he required models whose 'aura' must be the 'starting point for his excitement'.[1] Before the work is concluded, however, they drop away, and the 'picture is all he feels about it, all he thinks worth preserving of it, all he invests it with'.[2]

He went on to describe a process whereby each completed picture reveals to its maker a 'great insufficiency that drives him on'. This process sounded almost entirely sequential, and yet one of Freud's greatest achievements during the last decade has been to make the most outstanding works of his lifetime and, meanwhile, to create an art form which is enclosed and resonates within itself. Its independent parts, the completed paintings and etchings, thrive when dispersed, and yet they intrigue the spectator in another way when considered cumulatively. We realise then we are witnessing parts of one life and one pursuit. This could not be happening without the complicity of the people sitting. The studio life that draws them there depends on a chamber-like serenity and constancy that intensifies, as time passes, the possibilities that motivate the artist and the cross-references between sitters.

Freud has devoted himself to a mission as painstakingly constructed and as relentlessly pursued as Flaubert's intentions for *Madame Bovary*. Two years into the writing he told Louise Colet, and others, that he would soon achieve his ambition. It was, he said, to write direct dialogue, that is 'to write of ordinary life as one writes history or epic (but without falsifying the subject)'.[3]

From what there is to judge already, Freud's work will leave to posterity the vulnerability and potency of the people portrayed, in the manner of Rembrandt and Degas. The difference may be that he has taken them on unshackled, and so no longer protected, by the privileges and burdens of traditional society with expectations attached to roles, relative wealth, age and decorum. In some measure the people who agree to be painted forego the ordinary protection of a confidence-building self-regard. Once stripped, they and the artist have the chance to tip the balance against the orthodox control and egocentricity of the painter. The pressure is towards a perilous inter-penetration of exteriority and interiority, physical form and feelings, couched in the illusionistic, classical frame-work of oil painting. The results are very silent and very grand, so much so that they pervade and disturb most observers' own nervous systems. And make some people transfer themselves, imaginatively, to the situation painted.

Freud has engaged with nearly the same people in his art and life. Born 8 December 1922 in Berlin, by the age of twelve Freud was absorbed in drawing and by age seventeen had had a work reproduced in the magazine *Horizon*. The Lefèvre Gallery gave him a one-person show in 1944 and he was the youngest artist to be commissioned by the Arts Council to make a large painting for the 1951 Festival of Britain. The red-carpeted room with a tense standing figure of Harry Diamond called *Interior in Paddington* now looks stringent and adrenalin-filled in comparison to the other works.[4] Recently there has been greater variety in the age of his subjects, and as Freud returns to sitters he has known for thirty years or more, the images are less confrontational and more permeated by speculative brushstrokes within small areas. The majority of works have been shown and thus the British public has had access to what Freud has done for most of his waking hours. Even so he is described, enviously and antagonistically, as being an artist and person who is intensely private and inaccessible.

A succession of erudite and sympathetic writers, all of whom began observing the work in the 1950s or earlier, have now written cogent monographs and articles on Freud, most notably John Russell in 1974, Lawrence Gowing in 1982 and Robert Hughes in 1987.[5] Their accounts are governed somewhat by direct quotations from the artist, and certain remarks have been repeated and enlarged upon in the many explanations for 'The School of London' shows of the 1980s. Inevitably, the most used are those that suggest a bit of 'black magic' and a parasitic use of the anonymous sitters: 'I want paint to *work as flesh*, I know my idea of portraiture came from dissatisfaction with portraits that resembled people. I would wish my portraits to be *of* the people, not *like* them. Not having the look of the sitter, *being* them. As far as I am concerned the paint is the person. I want it to work for me just as flesh does'.[6]

It is of course properly humbling for writers who disseminate information and opinions about Freud's work, and likewise delve into the enclosed and elemental worlds of several other British figurative artists – Frank Auerbach, Euan Uglow and Leon Kossoff – that they should soon admit that it is the transmitted chemistry and magnetism of the paintings that fills our brains and senses rather than a correct decoding of the artists' intentions. The lack of exoticism or change in the situation painted further weakens the grounds for explanatory notes. In contrast to several of Freud's direct predecessors – one thinks of Giacometti, Balthus and Bacon – it is hard to claim even that he has invented a style. Freud really has shaped his painting to join what is by consensus great art by sensibility alone.

His is a sensibility that runs all five senses as if wired up together. Freud has the muscular acuity and concentration of a jockey or cellist, and something of their blinkered approach in as much as his normal method of laying pigment on with a narrow brush and conceiving each painting from quite a naive basis threatens to produce a performance that stays commonplace or mawkish. These qualities and the unimportance in his life of a formal education have made the necessary shadow of a self-critical view attach itself to appraising the standards, courage and feats of other artists. Freud has said that he has been consistently attracted to some dozen artists and their works, ranging from the Egyptians to Grünewald, from Hals to late Vuillard and to quite contradictory visions, Ingres and Rubens. Freud seems most devoted to those using subjects that he himself finds stimulating, thus Constable, Chardin and Géricault. Commenting on his choice of twenty-nine paintings for 'The Artist's Eye' show at the National Gallery, Freud wrote: 'One quality these paintings share is that they all make me want to go back to work'.[7]

At the time of his second retrospective at the Hayward Gallery in February 1988, Freud responded to the film director Jake Auerbach's question about artistic and personal responsibility with the confession that a life of absolute self-indulgence was his discipline.[8] The comment reflected Freud's awareness from early childhood that he should ignore external expectations and forego the idea of communal security or accountability. Incidents of danger and violence had made a strong impression on the child who grew up in Berlin at a time when the adults in the family circle were beginning to be worried about the strength of the Nazis. Although Ernst and Lucie Freud kept an ordered and affluent household (the barber came to them) they planned and proceeded with their move to England in 1933.

Freud craved independence and responded to Dartington Hall, the boarding school where he learned English, by keeping his distance from its own liberal organisation, preferring to spend time riding horses on the school farm. Moving later to Bryanston, he had his first experience of painting in oil (three pictures were finished). Freud enrolled in the art classes offered by the Central School of Art in 1938, aged fifteen, where he studied sculpture with John Skeaping. After three terms he heard about the independent East Anglian School of Drawing and Painting established by the rather fierce and conventionally outrageous artist Cedric Morris with his partner Lett Haines.

Freud moved down there in the autumn of 1939 and stayed for most of the time until he decided in April 1941 to go to Liverpool to try to join the Merchant Navy (he spent three months at sea before being invalided out). Morris's own work at the time was characterised by flattened frontal images, cartoon-like faces with exaggeratedly large staring eyes and prickly combinations of people and still life which probably encouraged a similarly mannered and alien look in much of his student's early work.

While Freud was staying in Wales with another student for Christmas 1939 he was already exploring subjects other than the haunting people he and Morris called 'non-humans' and, in a letter on the large page of a sketchpad, he reported his experiments thus: 'I've finished my picture of the crate of apples by putting a Welsh landscape in the background. I also painted a large monster [gap in letter for a drawing of a woman with necklace] and landscapes and more monsters and a street at night . . . I am doing a great deal of drawing all the time. I think my painting is getting much better and the paint is much more interesting than it used to be'.[9]

A pattern began in the early 1940s that demonstrates how consistently Freud has made his best works from people he wants not to disappoint or bore. The pure line drawings of friends like the quiet, enigmatic *Boy with a Pigeon* 1944 exude physical directness in spite of their use of the uninterrupted, unmodulated line identified with Ingres, which had appealed to Picasso in his portrait drawings of the 1920s and to others. More mysterious seeming pairings of people and things give a foretaste of Freud's unsettling vision and produce in what should be innocent subjects, like *Woman with a Tulip* 1945, an air of the opposite.

In the same years Freud was able to become familiar with pictures in private collections, gravitating towards the artists whose subjects and approach were most personal. From Kenneth Clark's collection he remembers the Elizabethan Saltonstall family gathered around a bed and Renoir's blonde bather and from Peter Watson's the pictures of Soutine, Picasso and Fernandez. Freud left for Paris in the autumn of 1946, settled down in a hotel and made two etchings (*The Bird* and *Chelsea Bun*) and the painting of *The Birds of Olivier Laronde*. When he met Picasso he admired his malevolence and remembers that the Spaniard reacted to his tartan trousers by singing Tipperary. The claustrophobic, wary look of European painters who identified with existential themes entered a number of Freud's paintings, with the result that a few nowadays (for example *Hotel Bedroom* 1954) seem compromised by a narrative sadness. The opposite happened in the single portraits of women, where their own delicacy helps sustain the air of revelation. Comparatively simple and convincing images are impossible to find in works by those affiliated to the 'miserabiliste' group like Francis Gruber (Freud went to the room of pictures hung at the Ecole des Beaux-Arts after he died). His best paintings and drawings slowly become barer and the vantage point draws closer, as in the tender *Portrait of a Girl* 1950 and luminescent *John Minton* 1953, until we see why Freud described his intention at the time as one of using 'the consistent distribution of information, and the difficulty of securing it'.[10]

This dictum might appear similar in approach to that associated with the Euston Road School whose main artists and their friends Freud knew from his first winters in London. However much their neutral observation of visual facts posed an alternative to a concocted surrealism, one can not imagine Freud continuing what William Coldstream explained was his own challenge, that is to unemotionally 'put' everything he saw in the right place.[11] Freud was open to manipulating the compositions and limbs just because of the sensual presence of the models: 'the effect that they make in space is bound up with them as might be their colour or smell'.[12]

Not only did Freud stay away from all painterly groups, he stayed away from the neighbourhoods that usually accommodated artists and intellectuals. The experience of everyday life with the sailors on a merchant ship in wartime gave him the desire and confidence to move to Paddington in 1944. The occupied flats in Delamere Terrace housed mainly people who existed outside regular employment – costermongers, villains and thieves – men who guarded their women and showed drunken, dangerous strength in the weekend street fight. Although Freud was stimulated by their company, he avoided a direct introduction of genre. For the next twenty years virtually all his pictures are of clothed friends and admired objects seen at close range. Freud explains he had a desire to confront other subjects, but a stronger sense of what he *could* do. And he was resistant to an approach that depended on a camera or on theatrical exaggeration. By contrast, in many of Francis Bacon's works (including *Two Figures on a Bed* which Freud purchased in 1953) the viewer is placed in the position of spectator watching from off-stage. Even the disturbing work *Reflection with Two Children (Self Portrait)* 1965, which Freud made with the aid of two mirrors, forces the spectator's eyes to travel up the figure to directly meet the artist's gaze.

Despite the lack of painted action, from the beginning other people saw Freud, like Bacon, as subversive and given that his romantic life was a subject of gossip, in certain circles he was seen as a threat, either because of envy for being the 'unquestioned Kohoutek, a new comet that blazed in first youth across the dreariest of skies' or in his father-in-law's words, a spiv who 'turned out a nasty piece of goods'.[13] The same people, unidentified, appeared in pictures for relatively short periods of time and were discussed according to a summary of personal characteristics like the 'wide-eyed' girl. Freud was taken to be like the soldier Pechorin with his Circassian horse in *A Hero of our Time* who moved stealthily through the woods, under balconies and through closed doors, admitting that 'as far as I am concerned, I always advance with greater courage, when I do not know what awaits me'.[14]

The obvious pitfall of this sensationalising view was that many of the people commentating on the work as *art* dwelt entirely on the appearance of the people portrayed; their desirability vis à vis the commentator's taste could be assumed to speak also for the painter's. Thus bodies were described as scrawny, sagging, creased and thus flawed, and only a few, like Gowing, found poetry in the 'angular awkwardness of limbs and the indomitable lumpiness, with which the body-shape is modelled by the life inside it'.[15] Similarly, writers dwelt on Freud's attitude and found it glum or honest and wondered whether misogyny played a part. Art historians struggled to make links with Stanley Spencer and the painters of *Die Neue Sachlichkeit* despite these being unconvincing either in terms of influence or shared aims of social observation.[16] A further problem was what was fashionably the avant-garde and concerned with the figure, whether it was De Kooning in the 1950s or Warhol in the 1960s, which was also art that deliberately denatured and ruptured the human form, either by gesture or by mechanical means.

One of the few critics who avoided summarising judgements and went carefully into the work was Robert Storr, reacting in 1988 to the first major showing of Freud's work in the Hirshhorn Museum (the only East Coast institution to welcome the work). He stopped short of suggesting Freud had added something to modernism, explaining Freud was more of a pre- than a post-modernist and identifying 'ambivalence as the subtext for all his work'.[17]

In a way it was a case of shedding ambivalence and engaging in the simple act of removing the clothes, the setting and the modesty of the subjects that made Freud's work start to become contemporary. The beautiful

Pregnant Girl 1960–61 was one of the first pictures with highly volumetric form – from breast to collarbone and jaw. The viewer was invited to have imaginary intimacy though denied a narrative reading of the relationship between sitter and artist. The physical candour of 'independent' girls in the years of 'swinging London' is essential to the three pictures of 1967–69 of the slender, 'purse-lipped' blonde girl.[18] They are not a triptych but the order seems sequential. In the first the pose and distance from the artist relative to the scale (61 × 61 cm) placed her navel nearly at the centre of the square. The legs are truncated below the knees. The golden highlights on the white ground are painted so sensually, they reciprocate the poetry of the human landscape. *Naked Girl Asleep* 1967 takes the entire form on the canvas, pivoted on the axis of the pelvis. In the final version of 1968 the girl is brought even closer and her arms are spread in opposite directions, pinwheel fashion, and a shadow lies under the whole perimeter separating it from the bedcover.

On the radio last year Freud told his interviewer: 'I'm interested, really interested in them as animals and part of liking to work from them naked is that I can see more and for that . . . forms repeated throughout the body and often in the head as well so that you see certain rhythms set up . . . I am drawn to certain things, rather like Eliot said "I am moved by fancies that are curled" . . . the insides and undersides of things I'm very often drawn to and when I'm working from a person I might use something which would actually be visible from another position because it's something that I like that would show in light'.[19]

Many of the strongest qualities of Freud's recent work are those he shares with sculptors. In the 1980s he kept several works by Rodin in his flat, including the study for Balzac with protruding stomach and *Iris, Messenger of the Gods*. The action of fingers on clay, the prodding, gouging, inverting, stroking, are not replicated in pigment, although the brush has this effect on areas, some impacted, smeared or built up by granules. Nor does the simulation of life stem from the fact that a few years previously Freud had changed from sable to hogshair brush and Flake white to Kremnitz; initially the loosening strokes had brought on a more fictional expression. To make things more palpable, Freud had to take on the mentality of a modeller. The results, in two dimensions, occasionally become extremely topographic, crowded with convex pockets, and flushed with lurid fleshy warmth. Then, as we are drawn into the work, softening the focus, we make contact with the poignancy and grace of the communicated relationship.

Sometimes a contrasting snakey line representing a vein or dark button on the upholstery enriches the identification of painting and corporeality. In general the naked people portrayed before 1985 were female, seen close-up on a diagonal line of the leather sofa, their bodies slightly swollen, breasts heavy. The position gives one to feel the artist could not help but conjure up the sensation of grasping or covering the form, thus stepping into the picture. The presence of the artist was made literal in the painting *Naked Portrait with Reflection*, 1980 that contains his feet as reflected in a mirror. Just as the experience of sculpture is normally bound to the place where we see it, these paintings start to bring the spectator into their 'room'. The piled rags entered as a natural reminder of the manual endeavour, and its moments and voices, varying in the undercuts and densities like the look of running water or tumbled linen: a refrain, I think, that comes closest to representing the artist's pleasure.

By the late-1980s the atmosphere was deliberately changing between one work and another. In some, like *Naked Portrait* 1988, the stark profiled alignment of the model, rather like someone on an examining table, was counteracted by the stretched out corner of the room suggesting the apprehensive atmosphere. In the best naked portraits of recent years the extraordinarily tantalising strain of night behaviour comes across; as with the cantilevered arrangement of limbs and gaps (as if the torso were steadied by a sculptor's armature) belonging to the blonde girl on a white sheet in *Girl Sitting* 1987–88. On the canvas Freud adjusts the matter before him with sublime delicacy. Eventually there are visual possibilities for getting to know someone better close to what the Bible wisely calls 'carnal knowledge'.

The interpretations that shadow these works are highly subjective, and many art historians would insist they should begin with admissions of our own gender and experience. Analysing Courbet's *The Artist's Studio* is the quintessential exercise and arguments about his intentions broke out afresh in 1988 with the publication of *Courbet Rediscovered* to coincide with The Brooklyn Museum exhibition. Linda Nochlin faced up to the question of 'reading as a woman' and went on to assign evidence of authority, submission and the allegorization of male superiority in the poses of the Irishwoman, Baudelaire and several anonymous figures.[20] Michael Fried, in a strong essay expanded in his book *Courbet's Realism*, suggested that one element of Courbet's daringly antitheatrical constructions of his large works was his ability to insert and enter himself and his artistic tools into the paintings and thus offer a view that the genesis of creativity as well as procreation lay with the female sex. Certain paintings are revealed to have alignments and contain linguistic references, especially sexual puns for the brush handle, hairs, pigments and palettes and their extension to bedposts, flowers and distaffs, elements that unlock messages. For example, because the orientation of the *Woman with Parrot* 1866 places her upper body closest to the viewer, the painter/beholder must tilt 'his' head 'sharply to the left as if in an attempt to look directly down at the woman's up-turned features'.[21] In other words he must reciprocate her seductive invitation. But when we come to compare 19th century pictures in which the female subject, before the easel, is the well-spring of inspiration leading to metaphor, we see we are far from the situation in Freud's studio. There the private conversations and physical nearness between artist and sitters goes into a compact which builds the picture day by day, absorbing the life that transpires, until nothing should need to be 'read' in. In general, Freud prefers to 'overwork' the paintings until they nearly expire.

Courbet, Rodin and Freud have all produced images confined to the genitals and immediately surrounding area. Within the stereotyped associations between natural elements (cave and tunnel versus root and trunk) there is also a shared arcadian peacefulness that because of each artist's expressive touch makes analogies to an organism that ventilates, smells and succours. The anatomy of Freud's lower bodies communicates in as individual a way as do the faces in closely related pictures. This is true of the agitated *Portrait Fragment* 1971 which was abandoned with only the centre painted and of *Fragment (Leigh)* 1992 which began as a full-length portrait. When the rest of the canvas was discarded and the fragment restretched as nearly a double-square, the couch and floorboards after repainting became denser and more cosseting.

When Freud contributed his views to *Cambridge Opinion* in 1963 the suggestion was that the spirit of the times, however pessimistic, was stimulating: 'When man finally sealed his destiny by inventing his own inevitable destruction he also gave art absolute gravity by adding a new dimension: this new dimension, having the *end in sight* can give the artist supreme control, during and such awareness of his bearings in existence that he will (in Nietzsche's words) create conditions under which "a thousand secrets of the past crawl out of their hideouts – into his sun".' The postscript inferred that this adventure depends not only on what is topical – the atom bomb, AIDS, etc. – but equally on the concept of mutuality of artist and subject. By releasing inhibition, the lubricant of sexuality, heterosexual and homosexual, dreamy and tactile, travels outside the metaphors of reproduction and life source into more risky and original areas of speculative thought.

The decade when he achieved 'a new dimension' began when the room used as a studio in his Holland Park flat became the setting for episode-long engagements with a few people, as many men as women. Freud began working over two uninterrupted stretches, frequently each of seven or eight hours duration, dawn until early afternoon and early evening until well past midnight. In recent years Freud has nearly always been occupied in making a large painting simultaneously with several smaller ones and his attempt to finish something ambitious has intensified the pressure overall. The way the people and furniture of his epic pictures move around the area of the large rectangular room, registering its walls, windows and doors, contributes to an even greater sense of life and, curiously, of imprisonment within the pictures. This happens in a mundane way as the long hours involve more 'living' on the premises with breaks for eating, reading newspapers and feeding the dog, as well as for the practical chores of painting, mixing colours and wiping brushes. Since the sitters are expending major parts of their lives in the studios, and the artist nearly all his, so they adjust their energy and emotion to each other.

Strangely, the first large picture of the 1980s, the famous *Large Interior W11 (after Watteau)* 1981–83 (186 × 198 cm) has, and overcomes, the weaknesses of the other work with artificial content, *Large Interior W9* 1973. As Freud was arranging the five people, he did so in a way which exposed his influence over them, from the costumes they put on to the fact of sitting closely together on a bed and 'sharing' their relationship with the artist standing a few paces away. The picture is most convincing when it is shown on its own, even in a slightly pretentious way as happened in the hushed room at Agnews where it appeared weeks after its completion. The proscenium effect of the floorboards contributes to the mirage-like effect, credible and vulnerable, whereas the plain func-tionality of the setting makes the costumes seem more like those from an attic trunk and an acknowledgement that the gathering was not an enchanted interlude. Indeed, insecurity spreads over the whole of *Large Interior*, from the people to the running water and the empty space.

Nothing so self-conscious enters the painting of Freud's mother begun in 1982.[24] She is dressed in white, brought into the close position of the foreground but held away from the surface by the lines of the folding chair. Behind her are the quiet, softly glowing panels of the window blind. She is evidently getting older as we observe her lovely hair thinning, but also girlish in her bare legs and light bones of the body. The repeated diagonal lines, lower left to upper right in the bed frame, chair, thigh and those in the opposite direction on the pillow and lower leg, together with the figure's depth evoke a rectangular box and a departure.

Freud never uses figures for compositional reasons and it is often the sitters who suggest how they wish to lie down or sit. The blonde girl stretched out against the bank of rags in *Lying by the Rags* makes a stiff effect rather sarcophagi-like except that she almost levitates in space. Leigh's body see-sawed between the green-striped mattress and the pile of rags contains a sequence of triangles that pulls our vision towards his centre and then out along the silhouette, giving a profound sense of organic and inorganic. Curiously, such a sense of substance and proximity Freud can achieve in the etchings, at least those dating from 1983. The needle scratches the copper plate in discrete patterns, frequently as facsimile representations with spores for muscles and horsehair stuffing mimicking pubic hair, with the traceries of the etching needles relating to the painted images as the dried veins of a leaf do to the live version. Where the swelling convex forms, like those of shoulders and stomach, emerge they read as much more brilliantly white and solid than the paper of the background and the ideas correspond to the jolting effect of the sharp 'guillotined' line of the paper edge.

In the past Freud's response to still-life, his favourite plants, textiles and books, produced fanatic and melancholy detail that intimated a chosen isolation. It still comes into the inert material, although the backgrounds are less frequently entirely monochromatic, and are sometimes enriched with smeared or saturated impasto or doe-skin-like softness or pungent red cushioning. A wildflower-like display of painting wipings behind *Ib and her Husband* suggests this 'landscape' belongs to her and in the early stages of its execution the radiator resembled a fence (it is still a dark barrier) and ultimately it is her face that is heavenly. A deliberate change between works according to the people in them makes some surrounding areas read as more obviously pungent, in a sepulchral manner like those of Rembrandt or Manet, and others belong to anachronistically fussy surroundings, stippled like those wall surfaces of David. What Lawrence Gowing wrote of Vermeer applies: 'The space in which Vermeer's figures are disposed, so singular by comparison with other painters' versions of his themes, is like a magnetic field. It is formed exactly by the tensions which the figures set up. The design precisely contains them'.[25]

Freud wants all his works to proceed as if inevitable. When he sets about making the bigger pictures, the relationship of the subject to his 'own' space and the necessity to foreshorten, especially the suspended parts, such as legs over chairs, as well as the strangely small scale of the heads, make planning the boundaries much harder. It is his custom to start painting the figure and occasionally to nearly finish before other areas of the canvas are even touched with paint, and then to revise the whole. Although he usually paints in charcoal or wash a general indication on the bare canvas, quite often the area left is too small and the canvas has to be extended on one or more sides.[26] A few works are abandoned since Freud dreads quoting himself. Towards their end Freud listens to the opinion of Frank Auerbach. Final adjustments come often not to correct what makes us blush, but to draw a larger, more disturbing point from just this gaucheness.

The advantage of using his lowish bed, sofa or floor is that maximum body surface and form come onto the canvas. After someone has been posing for a long time, 'I have to refer less to things that happen to be there and I'm in a stronger position to choose what I want to use'.[27] Leigh Bowery remarked on what happens from the sitter's point of view: 'There are parts of myself that I hadn't really thought about before but that I now really like, and other parts I'd felt uncomfortable about that I now quite like as well – such as my face, for example, which has never been photographed without make-up'.[28]

There are enough portraits of Angus and Cerith after their seven years of sitting that we should recognise instinctively the pattern of hair on Angus's front and the hesitancy and accommodating curves of Cerith. When the standing Angus placed near the skylight, leaning against the ceiling beam, raises his arms in *Two Men* 1987–89, his square, regular features and broad shoulders outstrip the legs that are perceived as two stocky units and therefore, in comparison, abbreviated and stalwart. His friend was inserted under the bed, as if in the undergrowth, and in the background *Standing by the Rags* 1988–89 forces a bizarre downward gaze and hallucinatory reading. Like Matisse's *Pink Studio*, it is very hard to 'read' the pictures as a unity, even one centred on character or meaning. The painted 'blonde' girl is more like a mythical temptress than in the original canvas or the small naked studies of her from previous years. The two men appear a bit storybook-like, reminiscent of Freud's illustrations to *The Equilibriad* (published by the Hogarth Press in 1948).

After a while one sees more. More factually, like the family resemblance between Esther and her grandmother Lucie and the same person painted on a green sofa and then in a butterfly jersey after a thirty year gap. Eventually the studio room registers things that happen, on the floor, against the doorframe, in certain weather, or as with the tiny *Man Resting* 1988, as if in a dream. A mission accomplished without the literary or cinematic effect of scenes.

The youthful people (otherwise a number are artists, writers, students) that Freud knows are never in danger of becoming the generic, luscious muses Picasso was addicted to in his mature years and on which he reworked fables using familiar types like prostitute, lesbian lover, old lecher, and so on. Equally, they resist playacting and charm. In comparison, Matisse's habit of engaging and dressing local girls from Nice, until they come over as picturesque and routine, leaves us uncurious about the guarded details of his libido. In one of Freud's earliest surviving drawings, *In the Silo Tower* 1940, the two bodies float over each other, touching lightly, his hand under her transparent hair. The composition is somewhat like that of *Bella and Esther* 1988 as is the distinction between one person addressing the artist anxiously and the other vaguely confident. The air-borne fantasies and long filly-like raised limbs of *Two Women* 1992 lets the mood hover into the realm of male connoisseurship, so deplored by women, and then out again by evoking something of the teasing sonnets of Shakespeare or of Thomas Wyatt where one's own passing life is savoured. Because Freud lets the daylight break up the surface of the skin and because he reads into the relaxed flesh of those dozing its natural tendency to folds, the young sitters seem older. And those establishment figures who in a traditional portrait might appear impassive and invincible seem to be stimulated into an orbit of speculation, eyes averted, that goes through self-doubt. Bruce Bernard as a standing figure projects the honesty and perfectionism of the living subject, made problematic by the temperament that extends to the flying belt strap and rooted feet and pushes against the confining walls in the head and the triangular area of the floor.[29]

Freud's people are capable of the 'soliloquising never-ceasing inner voice' natural to Americans, especially through constant psychoanalysis.[30] However, the soft options of being supportive and positive are meaningless. Travelling across barriers is encouraged and so are references to cultural and philosophical things as a means to gently combine guilt and self-determination. Much of the mood cast by Freud's sitters of the 1980s, old and young, has a literary parallel in the clipped syntax of the semi-autobiographical books of his daughters Esther Freud and

Rose Boyt.[31] The narrators share a dislike for the way the older generation makes apologies and the younger one suffers and conceals the shame of revealing needs, particularly conventional ones by controlled, sophisticated behaviour. An idea of people living longer but separating their self-awareness from any association with a life pattern that leads to old age, including parenthood, is something these paintings propose. Indeed, a revised and personal concept of liberation and responsibility divides outside reaction to Freud's view of modern life.[32]

Freud's reputation for exuding charisma and his aversion to quoting himself should make it extremely hard for him to realise self-portraits. He offers the opinion that, historically speaking, bad portrait paintings are all self-portraits. Just as it is difficult to remember the face of someone we care for, the opacity of skin and pupils in recent versions can act like novicane and there are more instinctive near-likenesses for Lucian in other pictures, for example the tiny study of Angus seated. The jolting, naked full-length portrait, 1993 throws the viewer off-balance.

In 1988, meeting Leigh Bowery after seeing his performance in the window of the Anthony d'Offay Gallery, Freud asked him to pose. He has so far made of him a seated front view, seated back view, reclining body with raised leg, a portrait, an etching, and the double portrait.

In an interview for *Lovely Jobly*, Bowery asked blunt questions:

In your work the pictures of naked women are always of straight women,
while the pictures of naked men are always of gay men. Why is that?
I'm drawn to women by nature and to queers because of their courage.
Do you like there to be a sexual possibility in your pictures?
The paintings that really excite me have an erotic element or side to them irrespective of subject matter –
Constable for example.[33]

The appearance of Bowery, whose 6′ 2″ tall body has a pliable thick layer of flesh, well toned and healthy, has strengthened the tendency to use paint as a paste, with density and surface so real that there is a spectre of Rodin's fleshy male figures, the first truncated Ugolino c.1877 and his succession of plaster studies of Victor Hugo, arm outstretched, surrounded by enticing, silent female bodies.[34] The pose of Ingres' *Bather of Valpincon* is nearly replicated by the back view of Bowery with the same turn of the head and the excitement of cloth against and near skin which argues for discovering beauty in oddness rather than in an ideal.

As the barriers are broken down, these pictures as a group acquire some legacy of punk, clubland, drugs and the generally non-achievement bound spending of youth, with its mixed attraction to androgyny and eruptions of supremely gendered eroticism. It is subtly different from the café and drinking club atmosphere of the 1950s and 1960s. 'My idea of leisure and lying about and daydreaming,' says Freud, 'was to do with that incredibly luxurious feeling of having all the time in the world and letting it pass unused – the sensuality of indolence. I no longer feel that. I feel that I might stiffen up and not be able to get up again. I never felt that leisurely, but now I feel less so. But I don't want any of that to show in the work'.[35]

Perhaps this is why he has been making big luxurious works with so much attention to the voluptuousness of the whole. Freud is sometimes compared to Degas. They share a fondness for horses and the covert animal nature of women that goes with avoiding the solicitous attentions of a moralistic female partner. The reason for Degas rendering his naked women, after the bath, without facial expression and Freud doing the opposite may be inherited. The photograph contemporary with Degas' 1893 *Self-Portrait*, shows the young Frenchman, cap held by lowered hand, making believable his confession, 'I felt myself so badly formed, so badly equipped, so weak, whereas it seemed to me that my calculations on art were so right. I brooded against the whole world and against myself'. It rings true then when the comment of Manet to Berthe Morisot in 1869 is repeated: 'He lacks spontaneity, he isn't capable of loving a woman'.[36]

Freud perhaps suppresses his naturally formidable and dominant self to edge others nearer to letting themselves go. Some, like the alarmingly aware little girl Polly, hold the whole picture. Each of the large pictures Freud has painted in the last five years comes out as though it might be the penultimate picture, and the threat of a flagging ability to paint or weakened mental powers now makes him work harder – and respond more spontaneously.

And the Bridegroom begins with a formal design, the $7\frac{1}{2}' \times 6\frac{1}{2}'$ scale allowing him to show the whole bed, its drapery and sweep of floor, so the bodies are raised and enshrined. Compared to 'real' life the skin becomes both gritty and glossy and the parts of the girl are over-articulated like a wooden layfigure with narrow waist. The drama between Leigh and Nicola is more mesmerising because of the unknown role of the artist, the missing facts of witnessing something. Except that like Géricault's *Raft of the Medusa*, which all observers see as ludicrous from a documentary point of view, the invented version can compensate by being a substitute for us all 'lost at sea, washed between hope and despair. Catastrophe has become art; that is after all what it is for'.[37] The nearest comparison in art to Freud's life in the London studio is Velazquez and his court of Philip IV. 'I believe in Velazquez', says Lucian Freud, 'more completely than any other artist whose work is alive for me. I understand Ortega y Gasset's strange remark on first seeing Las Meninas: "This isn't art, it's life perpetuated"'.[38]

1. 'Lucian Freud, some thoughts on painting', *Encounter*, July 1954. The text was written in conversation with David Sylvester.

2. Ibid.

3. 'The Letters of Gustave Flaubert 1830–1854', edited by Francis Steegmuller, Harvard University Press, Cambridge, Mass. and London, 1980, p.182.

4. The Arts Council invited works by 12 sculptors and by 60 painters who were asked to work on a scale not less than 45″ × 60″ on a subject of their choice. The project produced memorable pieces from Victor Pasmore's *Snowstorm* to Prunella Clough's *Lowestoft Harbour* but in comparison to Freud's work most of the pictures appear schematic and cluttered.

5. See Bibliography. *The New Yorker* plans to publish a piece by John Richardson.

6. John Russell, *Lucian Freud*, Arts Council of Great Britain, 1974; Lawrence Gowing, *Lucian Freud*, Thames and Hudson, London 1982, pp.190–91; Robert Hughes, *Lucian Freud Paintings*, The British Council, 1987 and Thames and Hudson, London 1987 and 1993.

7. 'Lucian Freud. The Artist's Eye', The National Gallery London, June-August 1987.

8. Transcript of interview with Jake Auerbach, BBC 2, May 1988 recorded at the Hayward Gallery.

9. Lucian Freud to Cedric Morris, Betws-y-Coed, Wales, undated, Tate Archives (the letter written on large drawing paper refers to the painting *Box of Apples in Wales*, 1939)

10. Gowing, p.81

11. Coldstream in 1937 in a letter to Dr John Rake in the Tate Archives. Coldstream insisted 'painting is the exploitation of vision not of material ... As an object on the canvas flapping on the stretcher is obviously unsatisfactory'. Freud was puzzled that Coldstream could work on a slightly curved surface.

12. *Encounter*

13. John Russell, *The Sunday Times*, 27 January 1974. Jacob Epstein to his daughter Peggy-Jean, 17 January 1955, Tate Archives.

14. Mikhail Lermontov, *A Hero of Our Time*, Doubleday, Garden City, New York, 1956, p.194

15. Gowing, p.189. Critics of the generation first writing in the late 1960s, like Richard Cork, reacted to the 1974 retrospective by protesting that Freud's means were not contemporary and that like other British artists of the 1940s he 'back-pedalled towards naturalism at a time when New York was busy revolutionising the whole concept of an easel painting' (*Evening Standard*, 7 February 1974). Several British critics have quite dramatically changed their view on whether Freud is dealing with authentic life experience or a minority interest (see W. Januszczak, *The Guardian*, 5 February 1988 and *Art Review*, June 1993 for examples). The most violent reaction was that of several French critics who saw 'le comptable morose de nus de baudouche soufflée ... et de visages aux chairs faisandées' and described him as 'un pompier de l'horreur' (*Le Matin*, 5 January 1988 and *Le Monde*, 23 December 1987).

16. The article 'Two Painters' by David Sylvester in *Britain Today*, June 1950 explains that Spencer and Freud share sharply defined forms but 'Spencer is Flemish and quaint ... His world is not authentic'.

17. Robert Storr, *Art in America*, May 1988.

18. Gowing, p.150.

19. William Feaver interviewing Lucian Freud, recorded for BBC Radio 3, 10 December 1991, produced by Judith Bumpus. The quotation from *Preludes IV* continues:
'Around these images, and cling: The notion of some infinitely gentle Infinitely suffering thing.'

20. Linda Nochlin, *Courbet's Real Allegory: Rereading 'The Painter's Studio'*, *Courbet Reconsidered*, The Brooklyn Museum, 1988

21. Michael Fried, 'Courbet's Femininity', *Courbet Reconsidered*, op.cit. and *Courbet's Realism*, Cornell University Press, 1990, p.204.

22. Lucian Freud, *Cambridge Opinion*, 1963

23. *Large Interior* follows the composition of Watteau's *Pierrot Content* which is in the Thyssen-Bornemisza Collection. In 'Lucian Freud: a little help from his friends', *The Sunday Times*, 6 November 1983, Gowing identifies the adult sitters.

24. Lucie Brasch (1896–1989) appears in *Large Interior W9*, 1973 and then in a series of paintings of her reclining on a bed, most of which were shown at the exhibition at Anthony d'Offay Gallery in 1978. The artist also drew her just after she died.

25. Lawrence Gowing, *Vermeer*, Faber & Faber, London 1952, pp. 35–36

26. Lately Freud has freely brushed-in the intended composition and then radically revised his ideas several times in the first few weeks.

27. Feaver, op cit.

28. Leigh Bowery, *The Independent*, 19 September 1991.

29. For example, the 1988 portraits of Susie are of someone then 18 years old.

30. John Updike, *Memories of the Ford Administration*, Hamish Hamilton, 1992, p. 122.

31. Rose Boyt is author of *Sexual Intercourse* and *Rose* (published by Jonathan Cape) and Esther Freud of *Hideous Kinky* and *Peerless Flats* (Hamish Hamilton).

32. See Waldemar Januszczak, *Art Review*, June 1993, p.32. Januszczak argues that Freud's art 'is far too privileged to be important. Above all, its universality is circumscribed by its lack of sentimentality'.

33. 'Leigh Bowery in conversation with Lucian Freud', *Lovely Jobly*, vol.ii., no.iii, 1991; reprinted in *The Independent*, 11 January 1992.

34. See reproductions in Catherine Lampert, *The Drawings and Sculpture of Rodin*, 1986, Yale University Press.

35. Bowery, op cit. – the quotation is slightly altered here.

36. *Lettres*, Degas 1945, CLVII, pp.178–79; Degas Letters 1947, no.170, p.171. Freud has referred often to Degas and kept the strange work of three girls holding hands, *Peasant Girls Bathing in the Sea toward Evening* 1875–76 in his flat for a while. Morisot, 1950, p.31, quoted in Degas exhibition catalogue, Paris, Ottawa and New York, 1988.

37. Julian Barnes, *History of the World in 10½ Chapters*, Jonathan Cape, 1989, p.135.

38. Andrew Graham-Dixon, 'Velazquez: the greatest living artist', *Vogue*, March 1990.

1

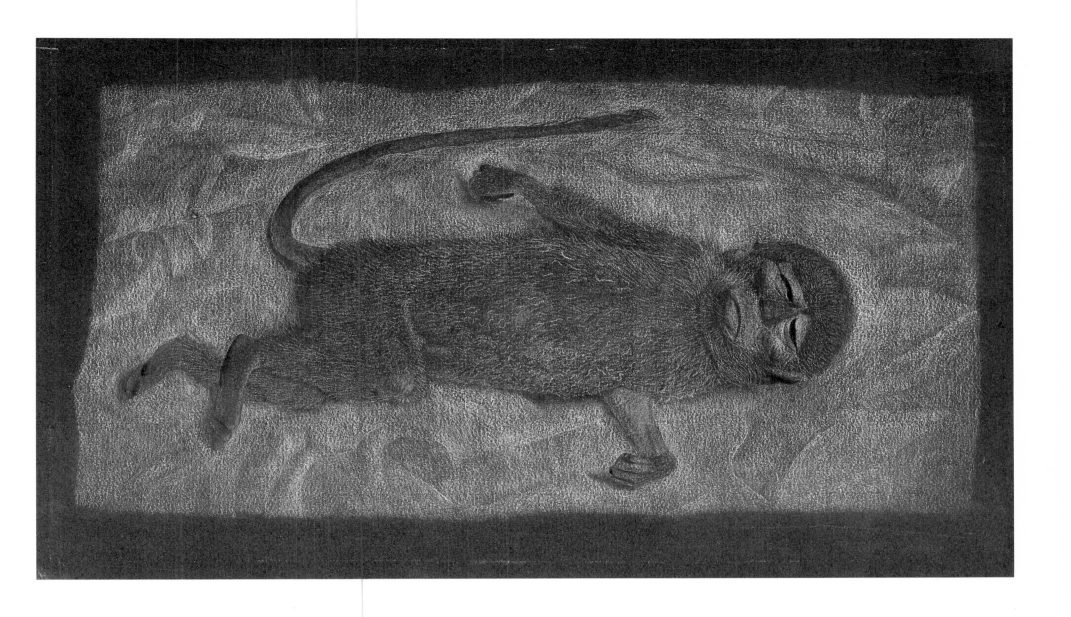

8

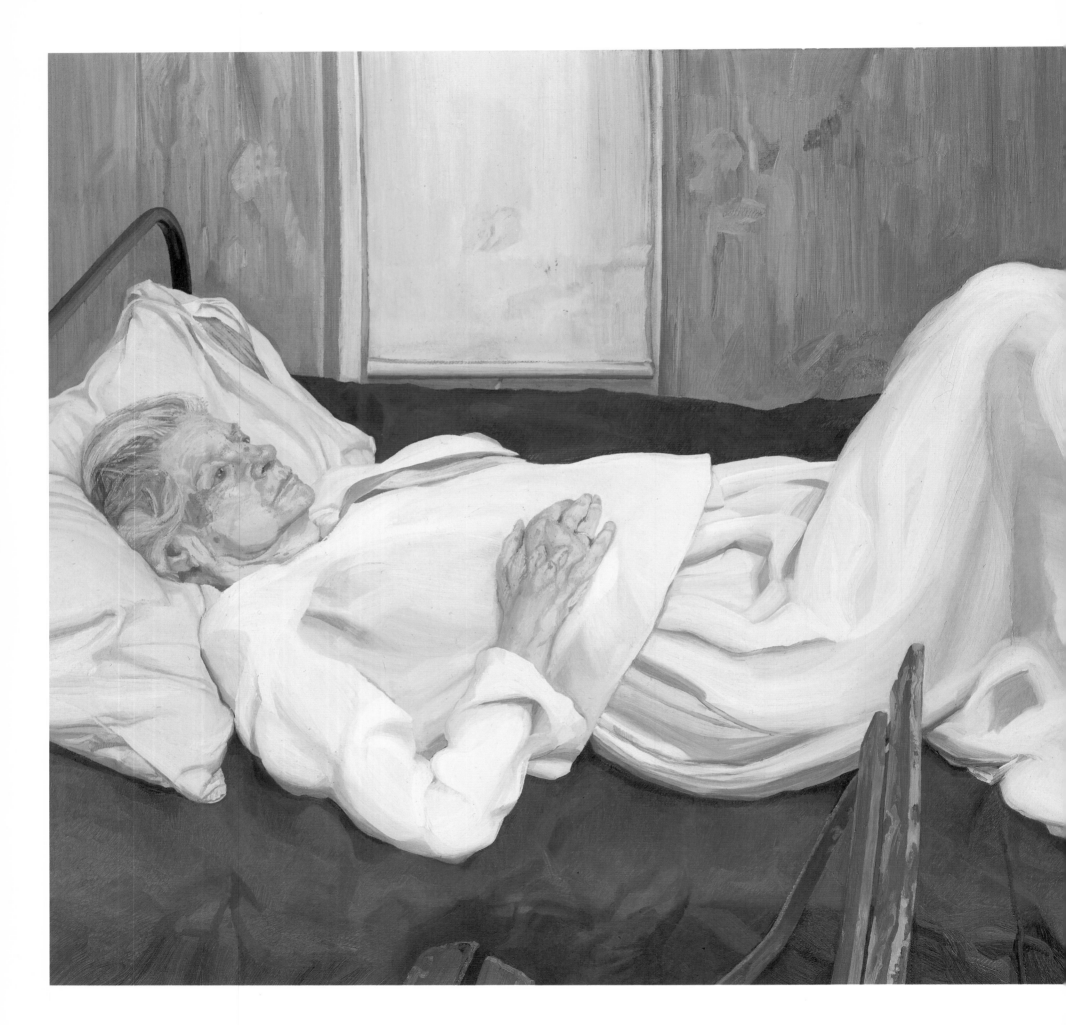

18

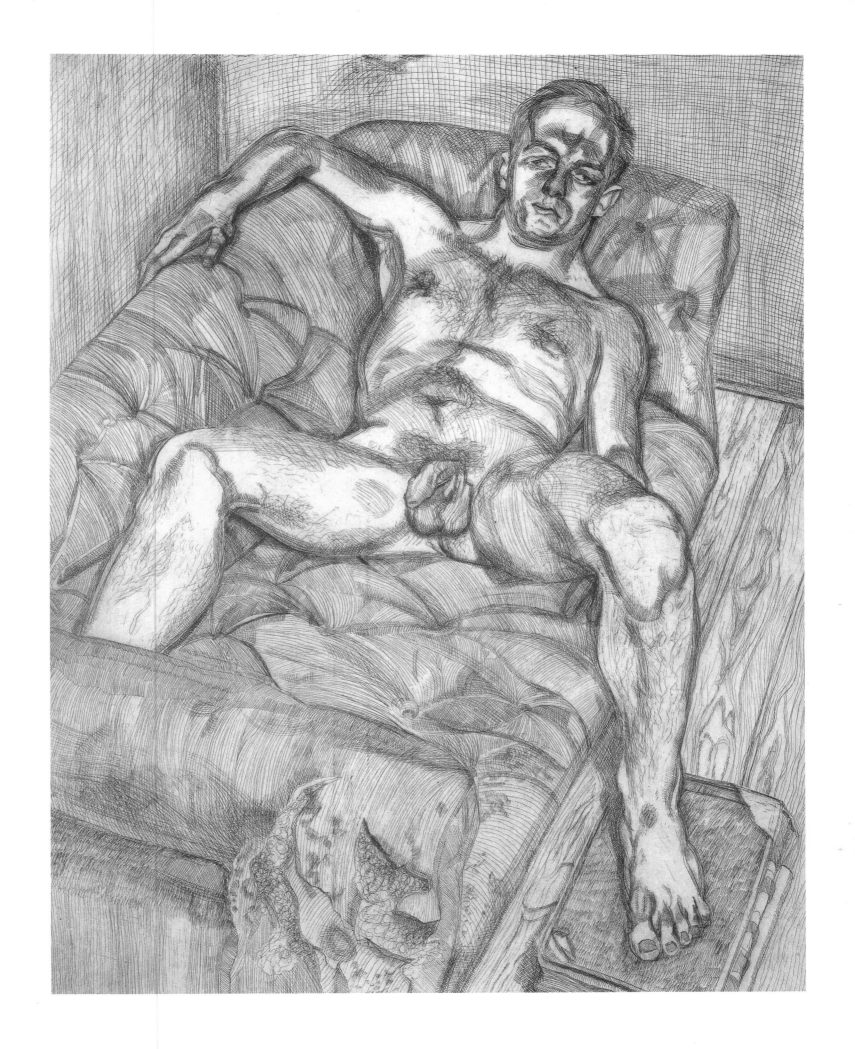

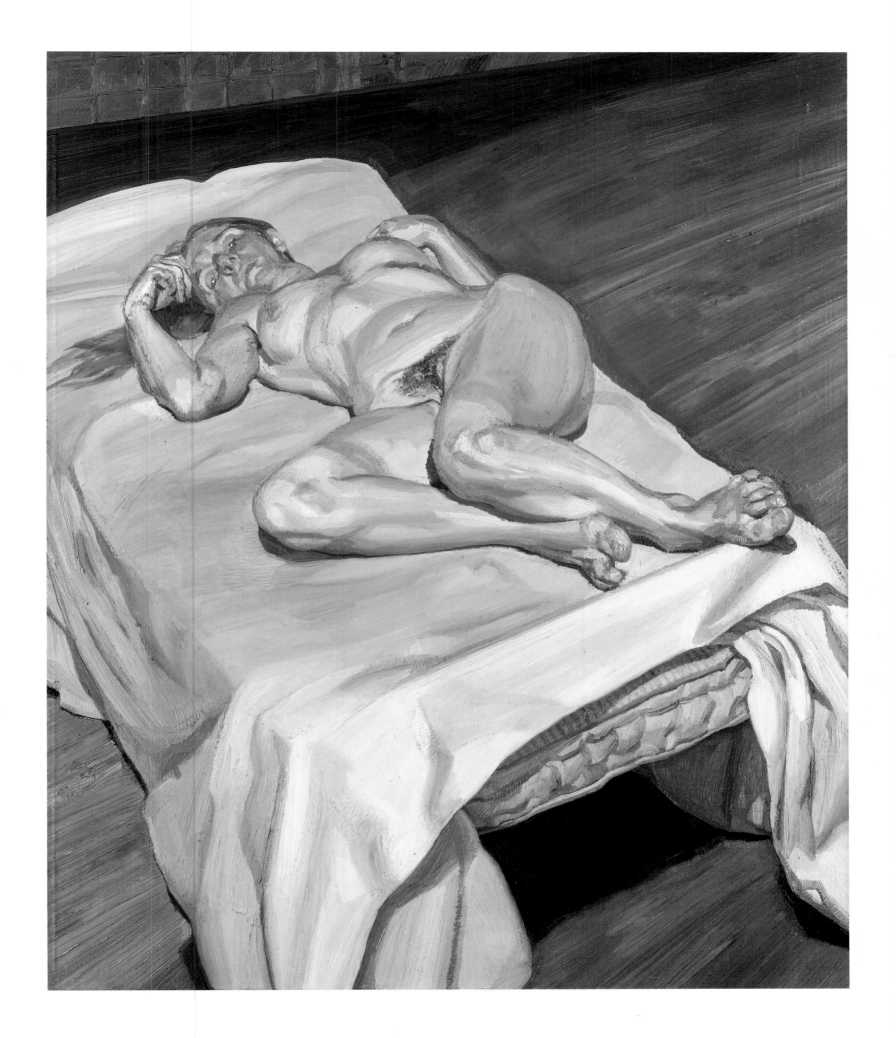

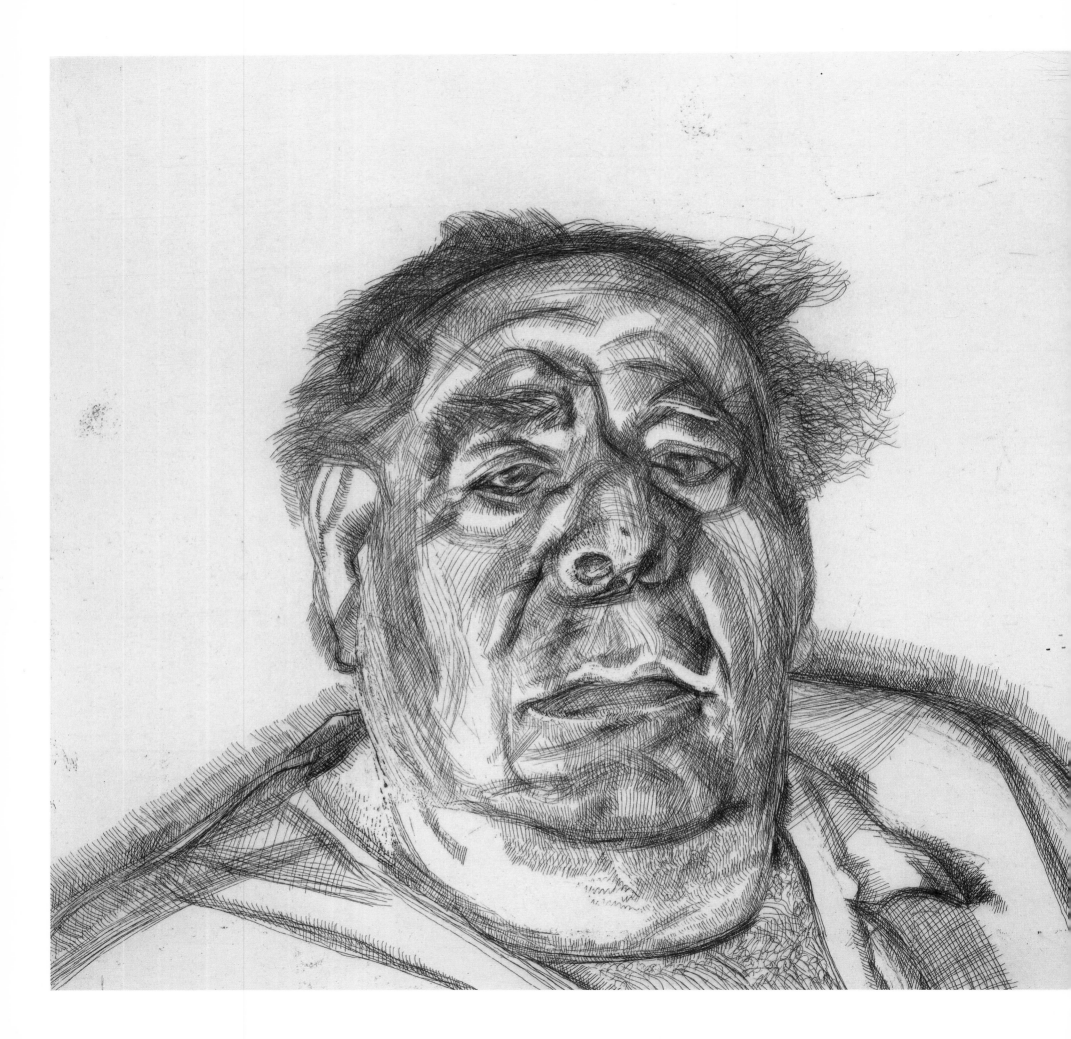

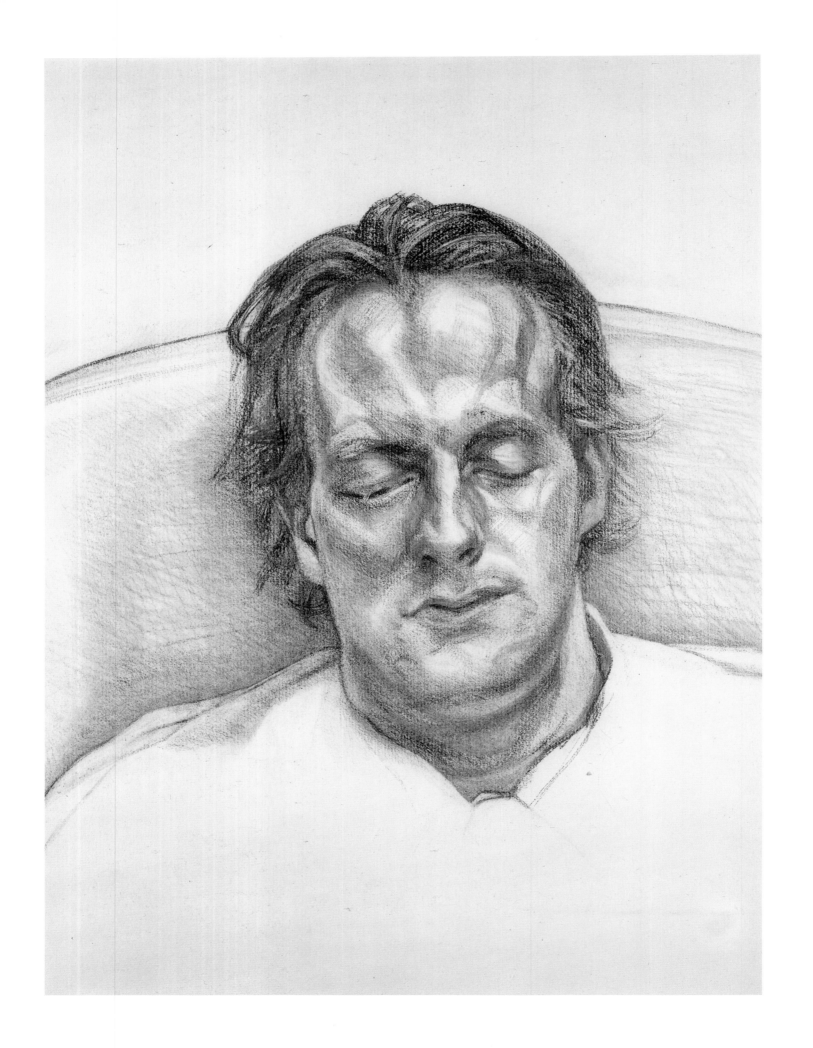

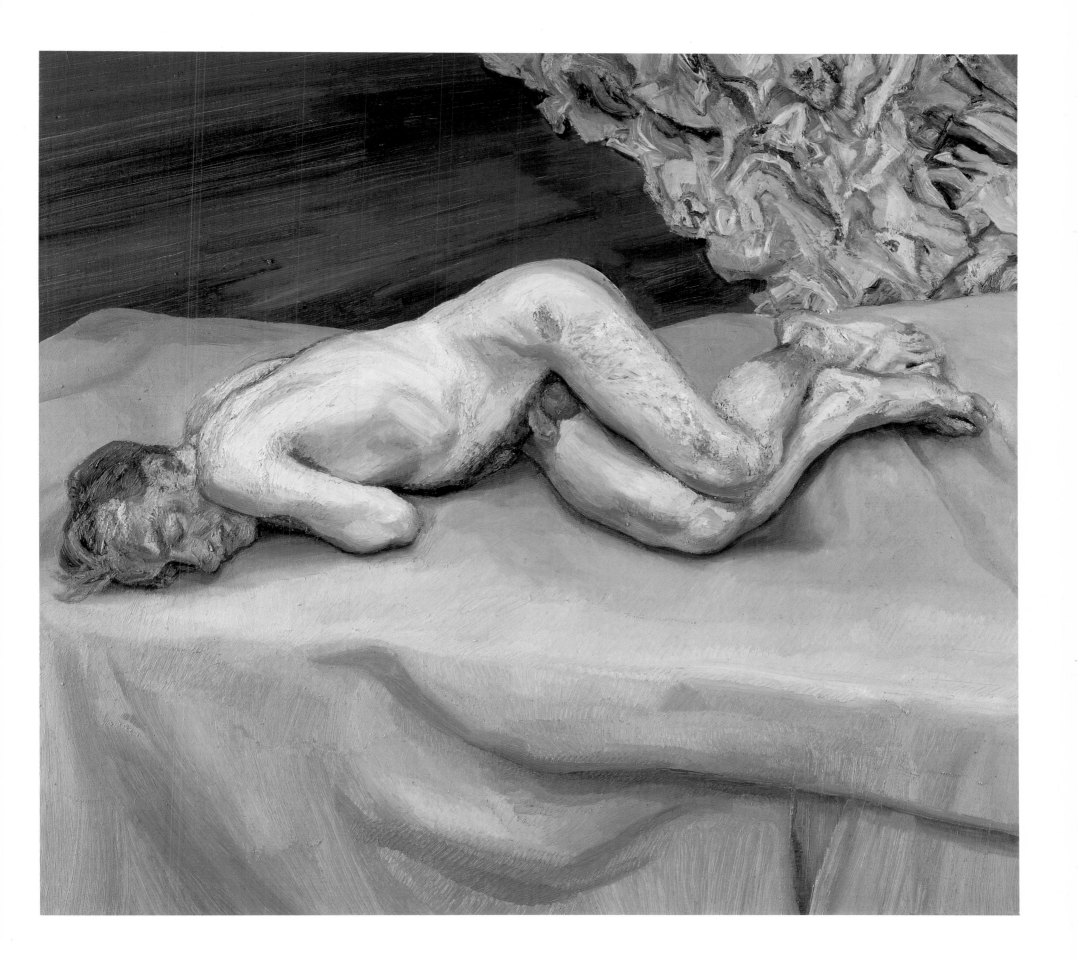

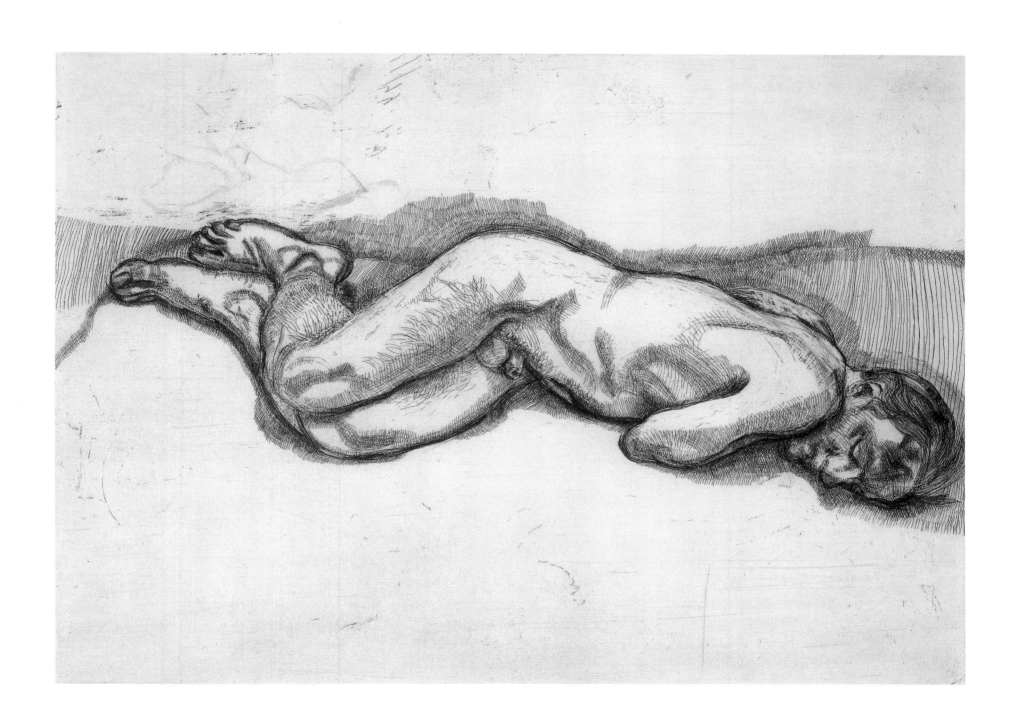

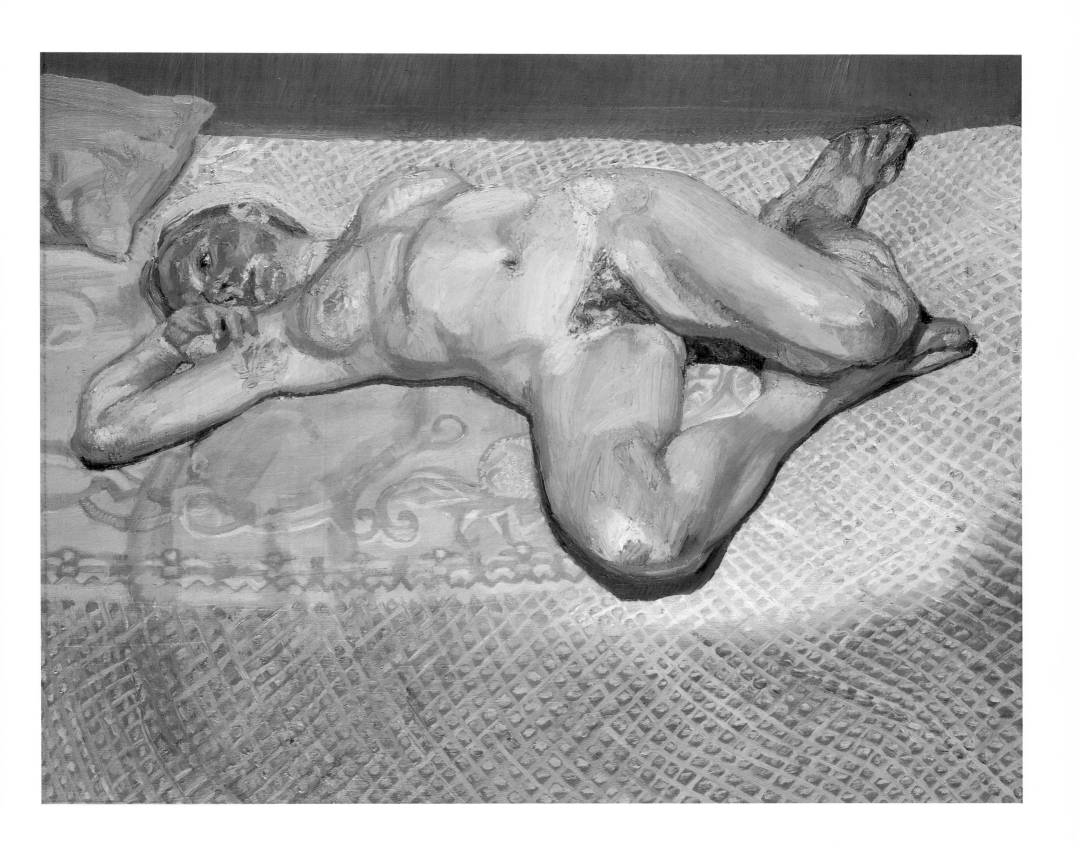

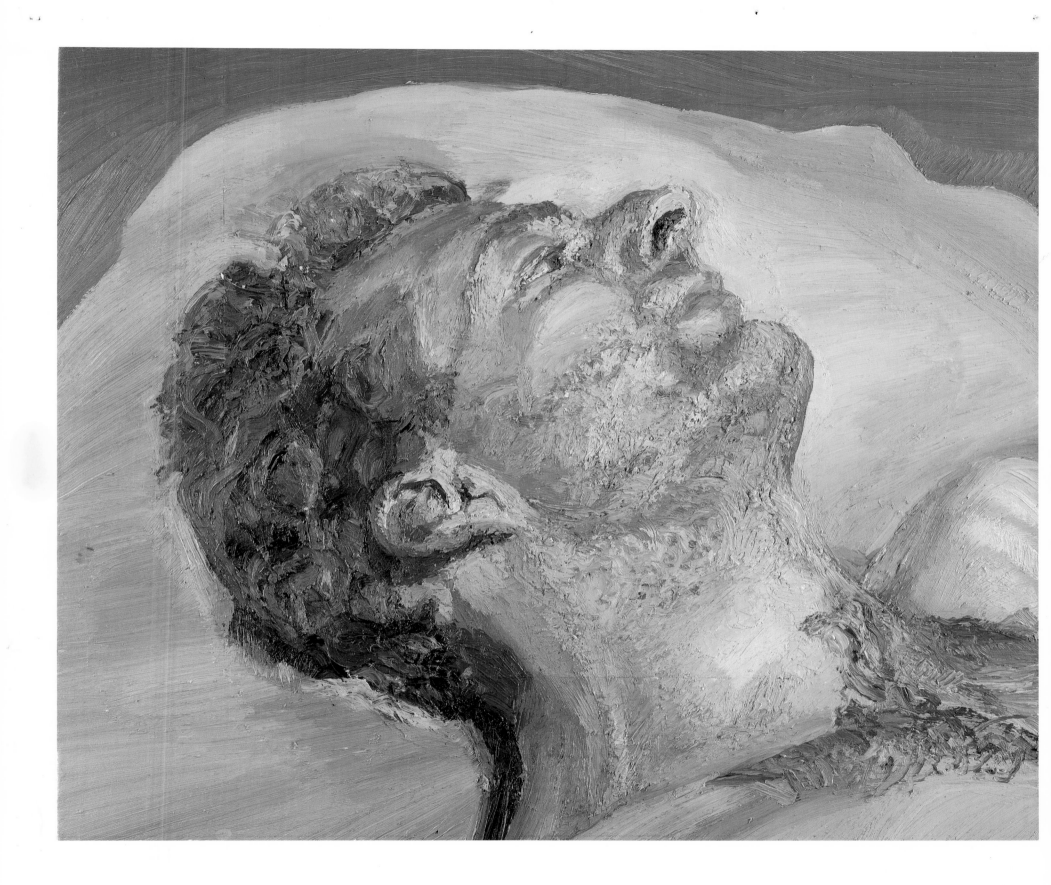

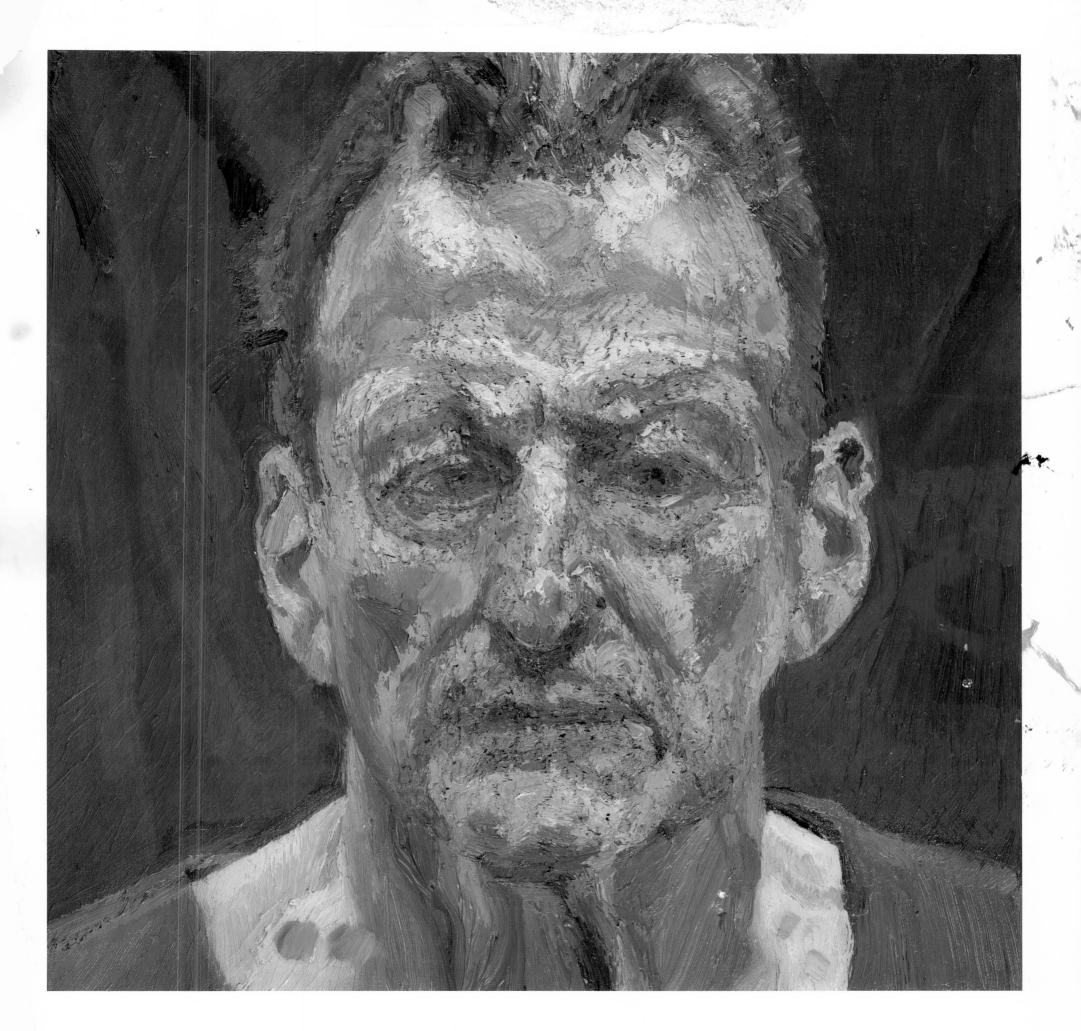

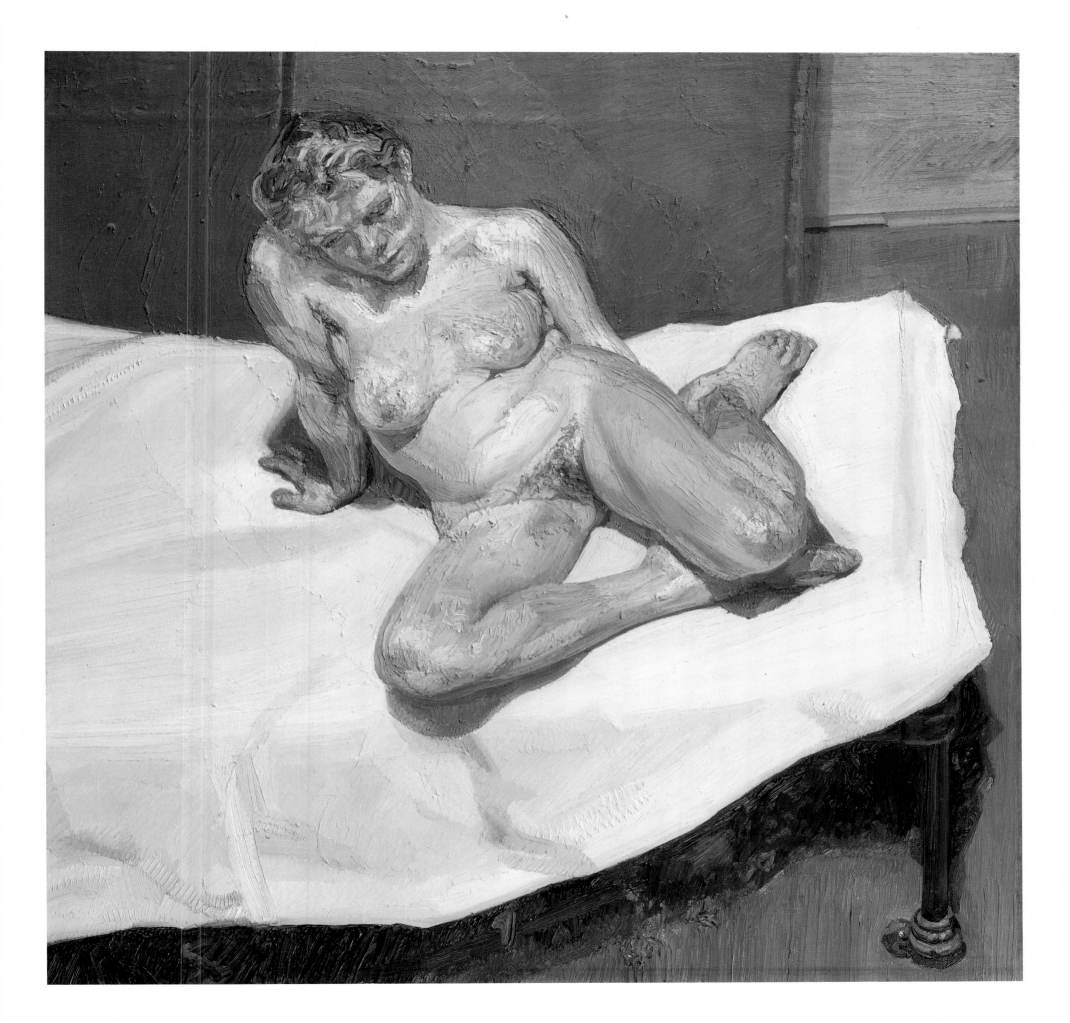

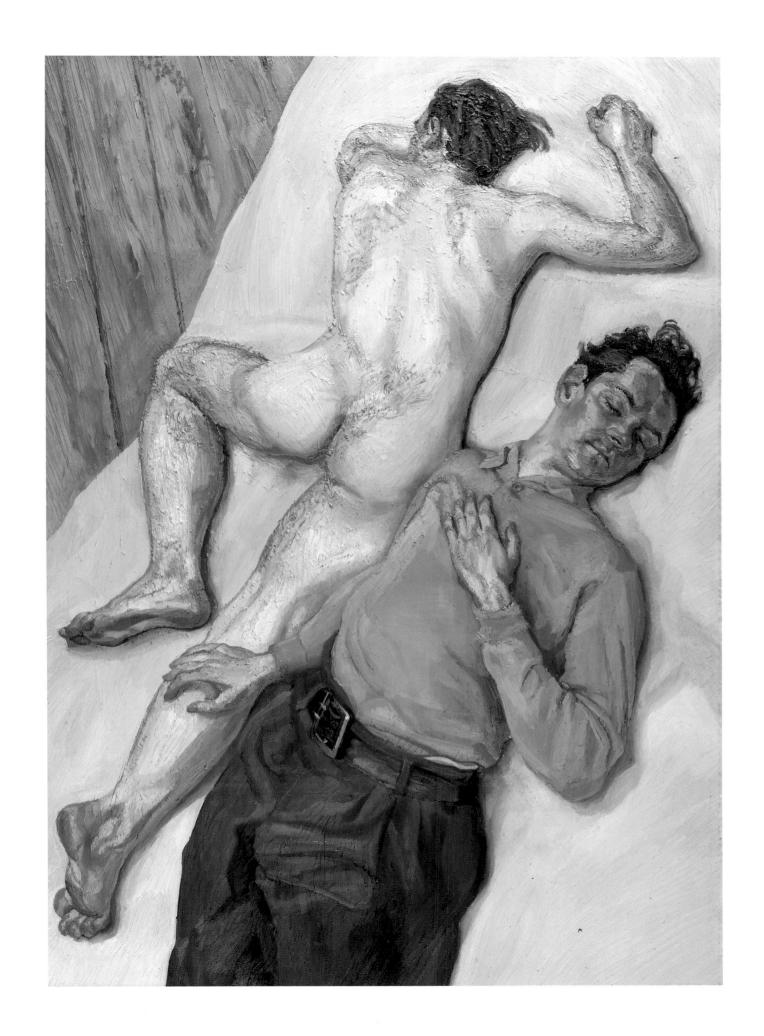

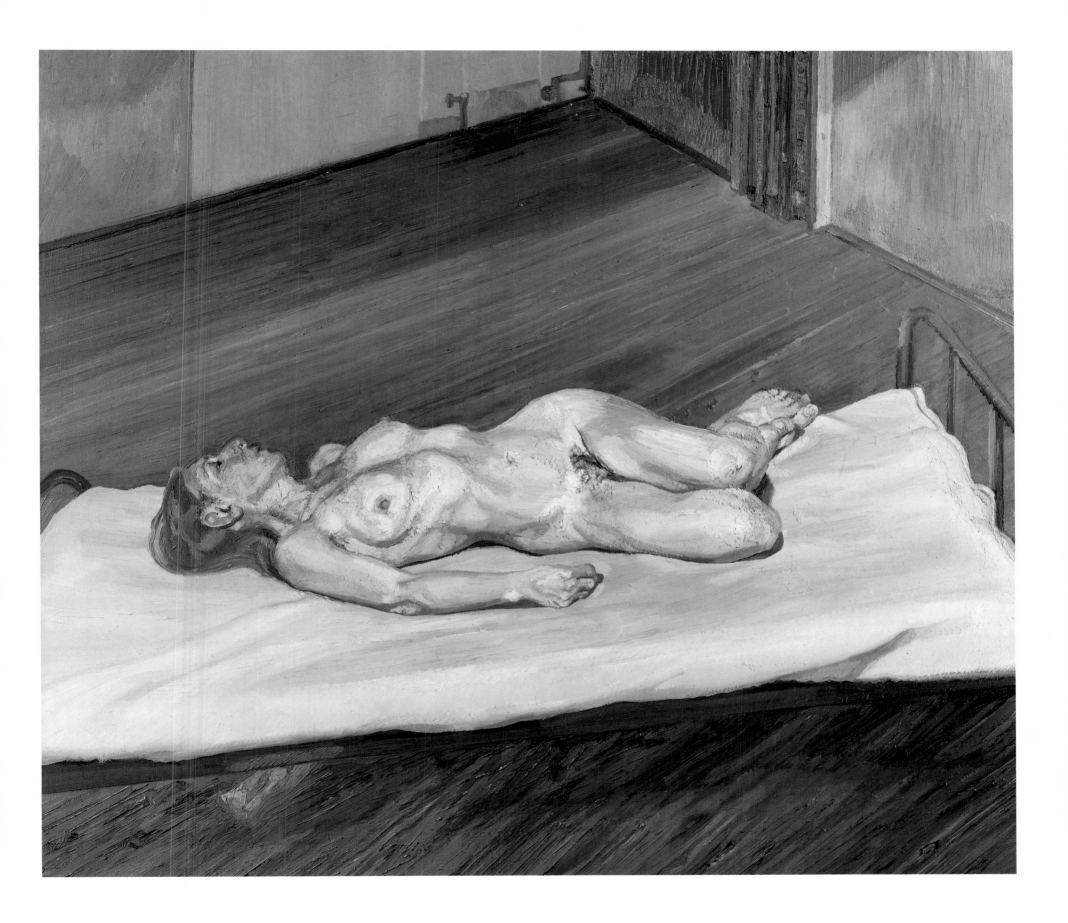

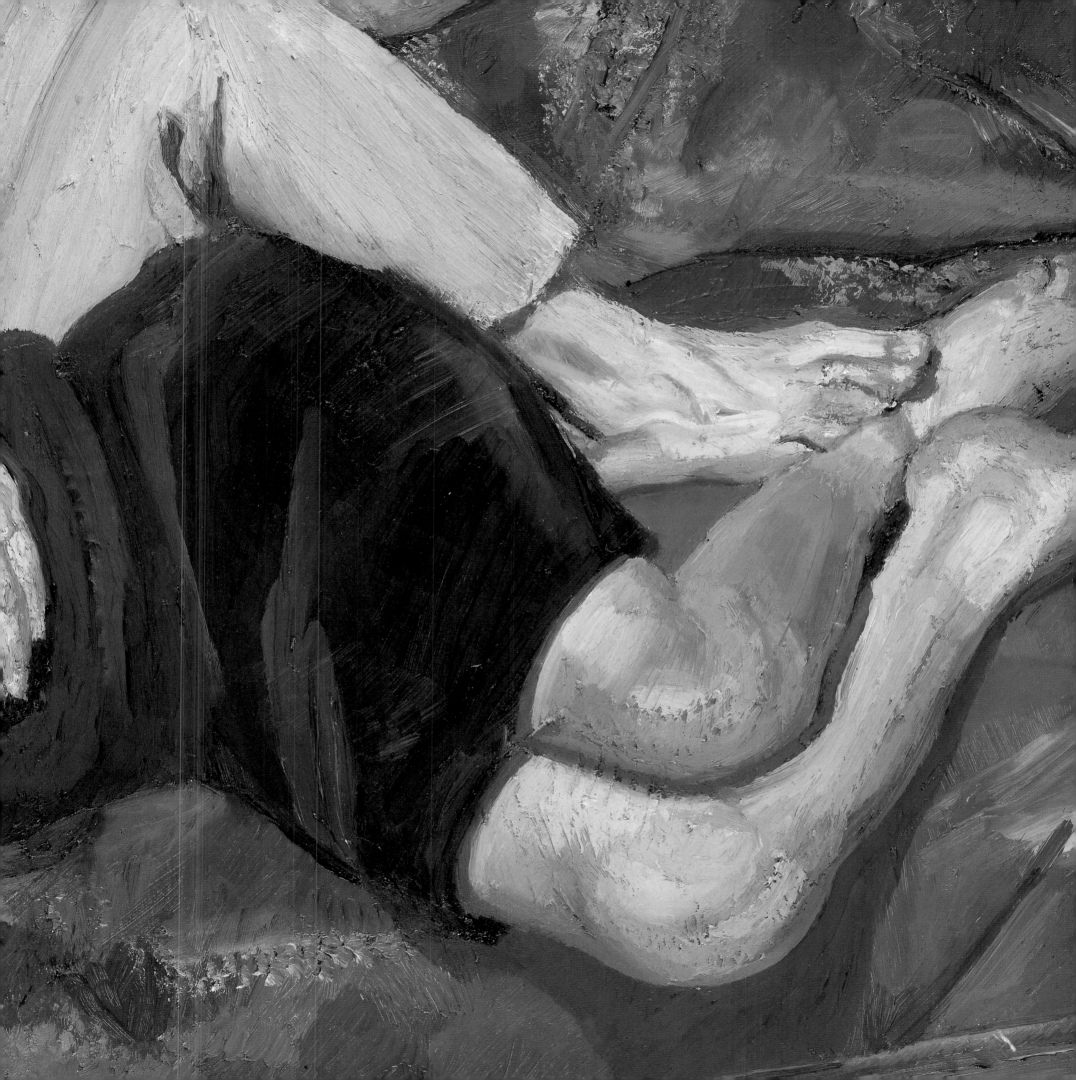

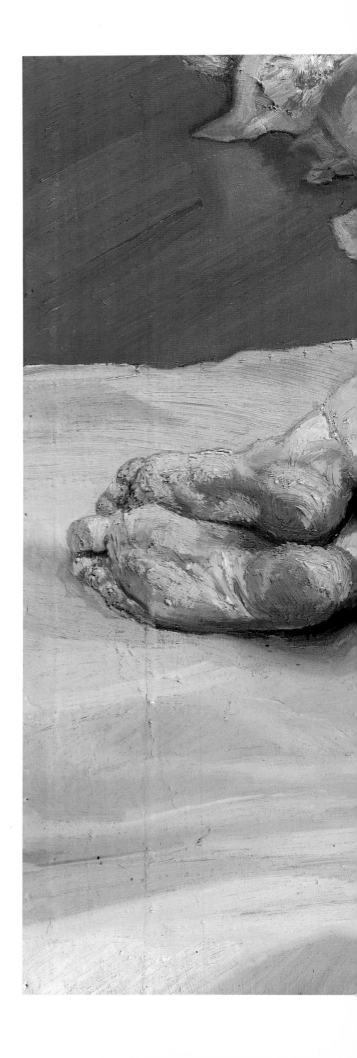

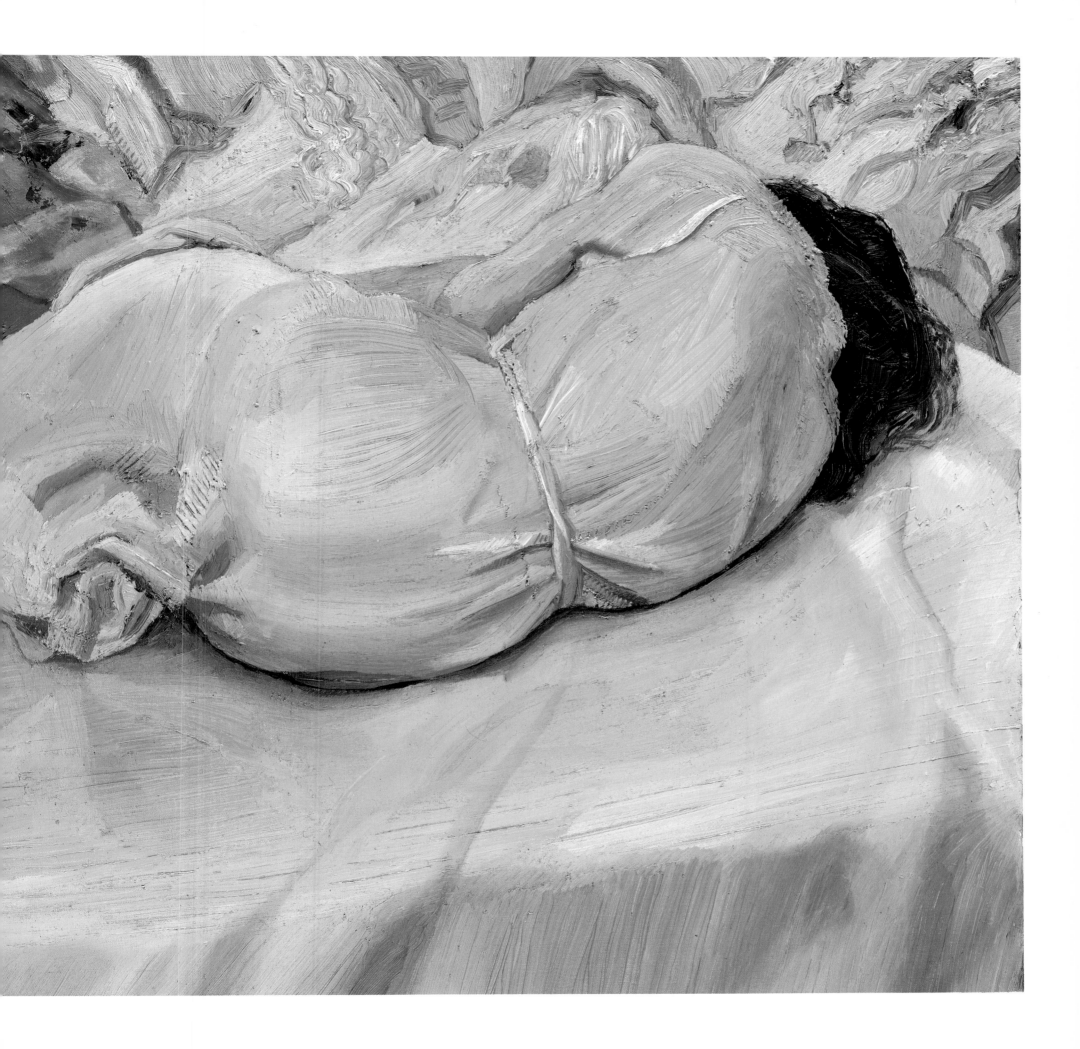

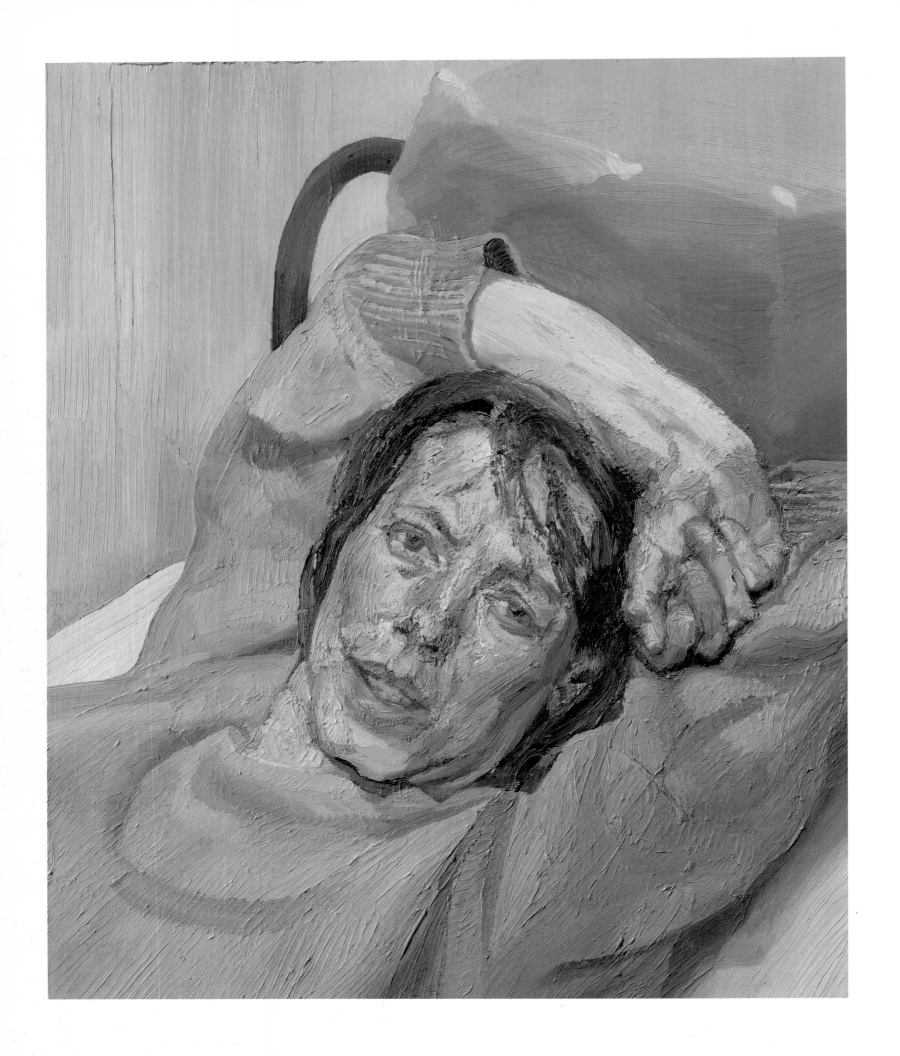

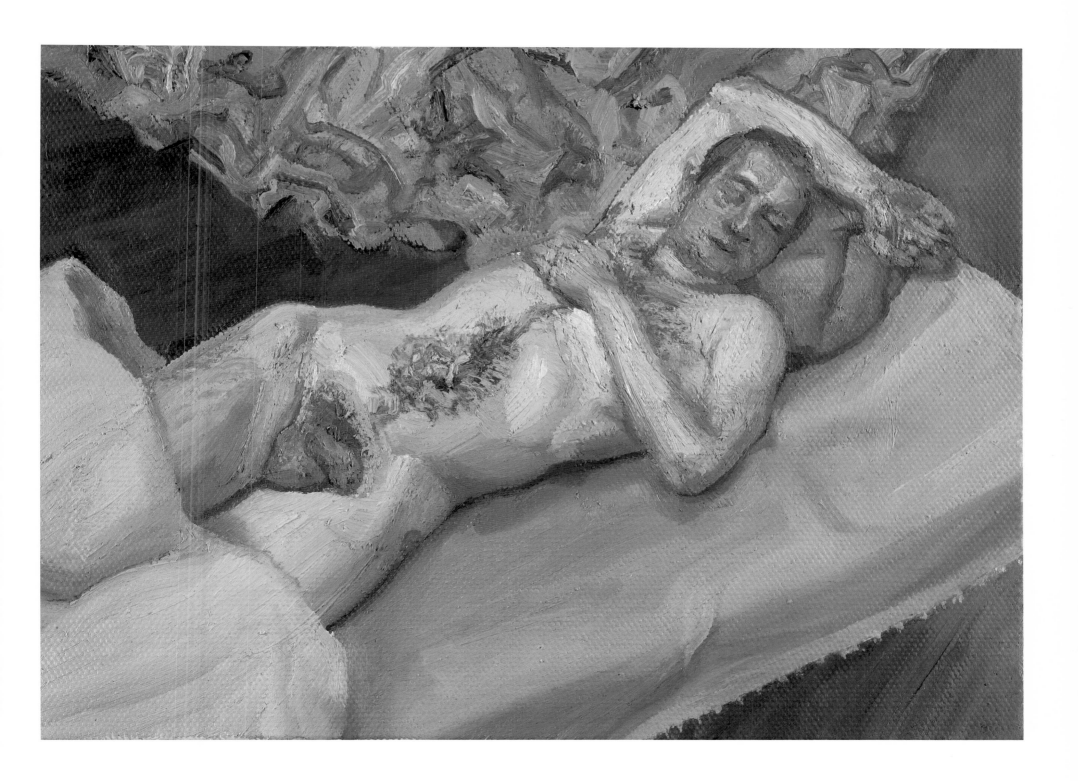

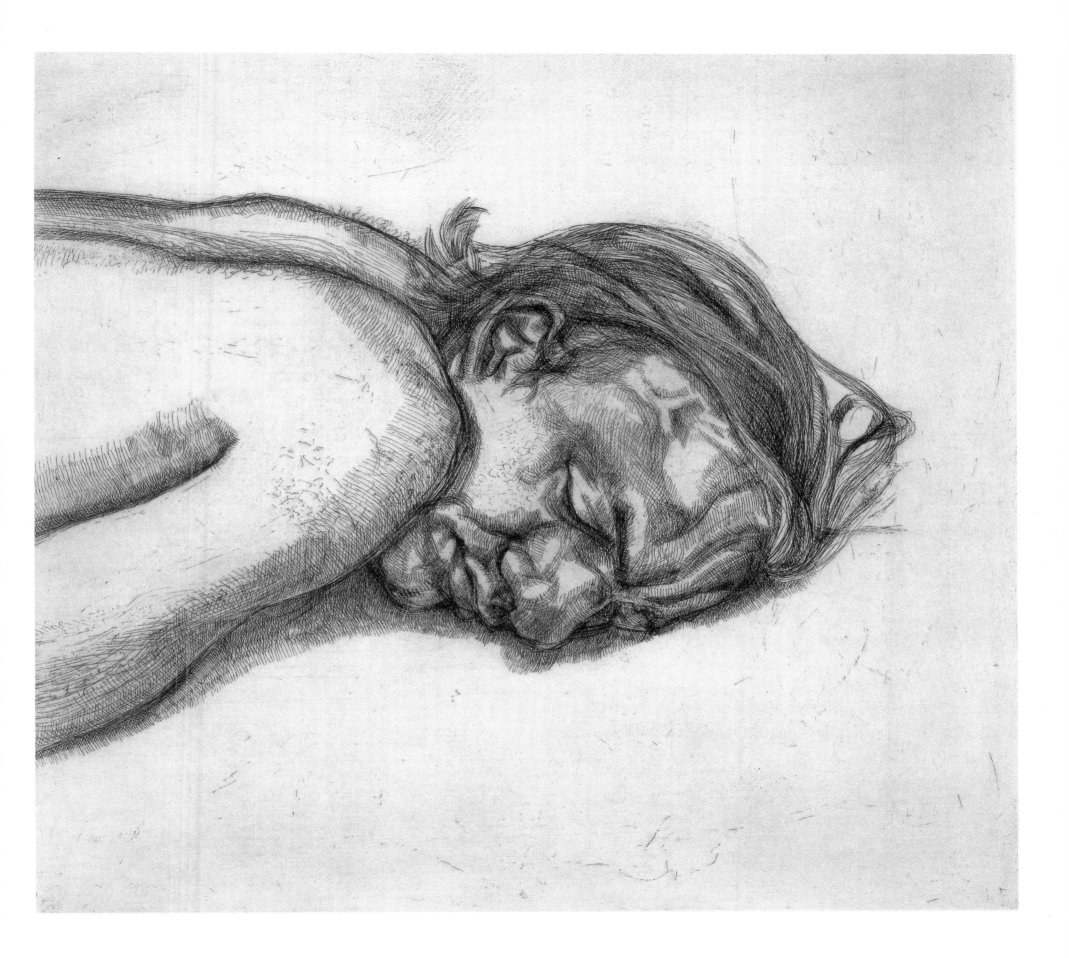

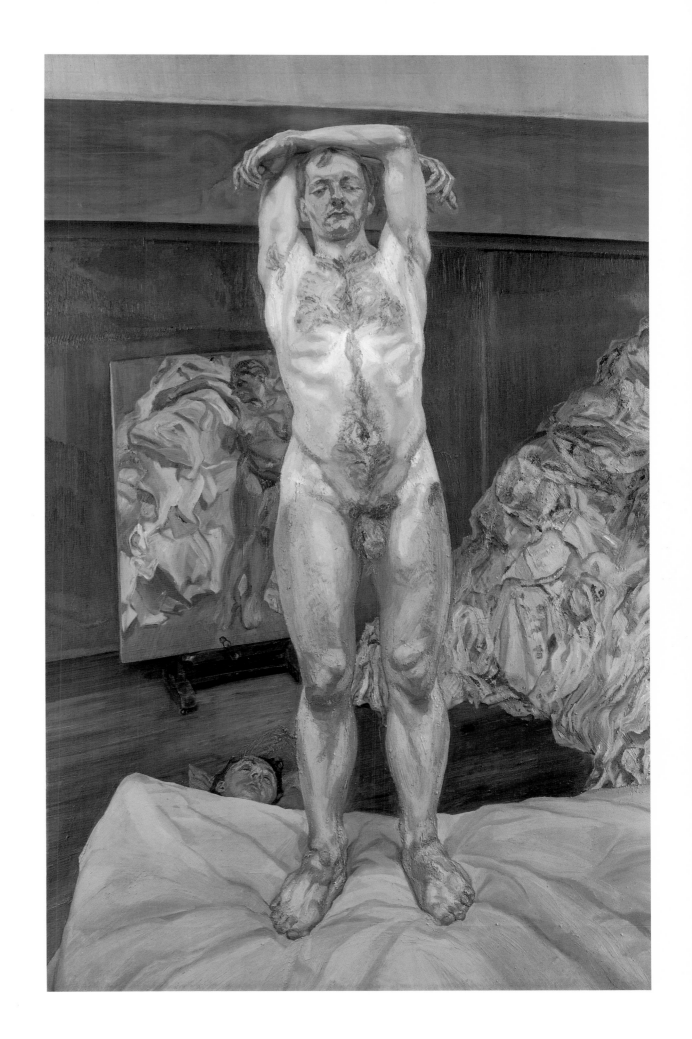

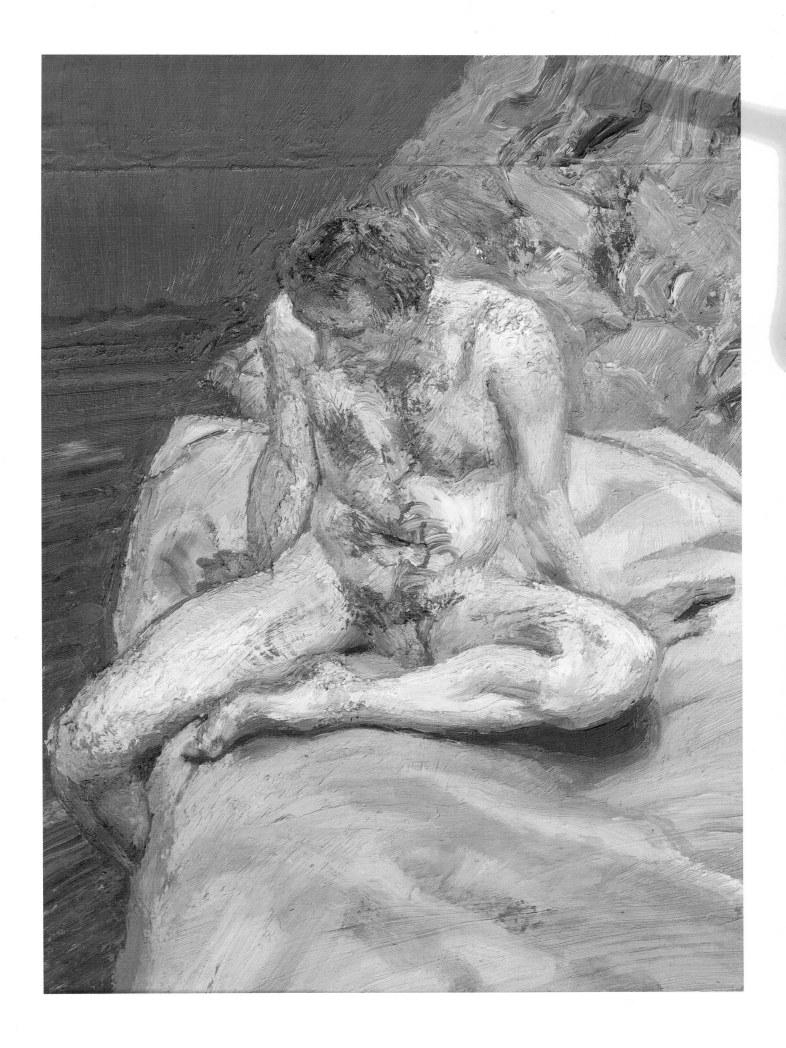

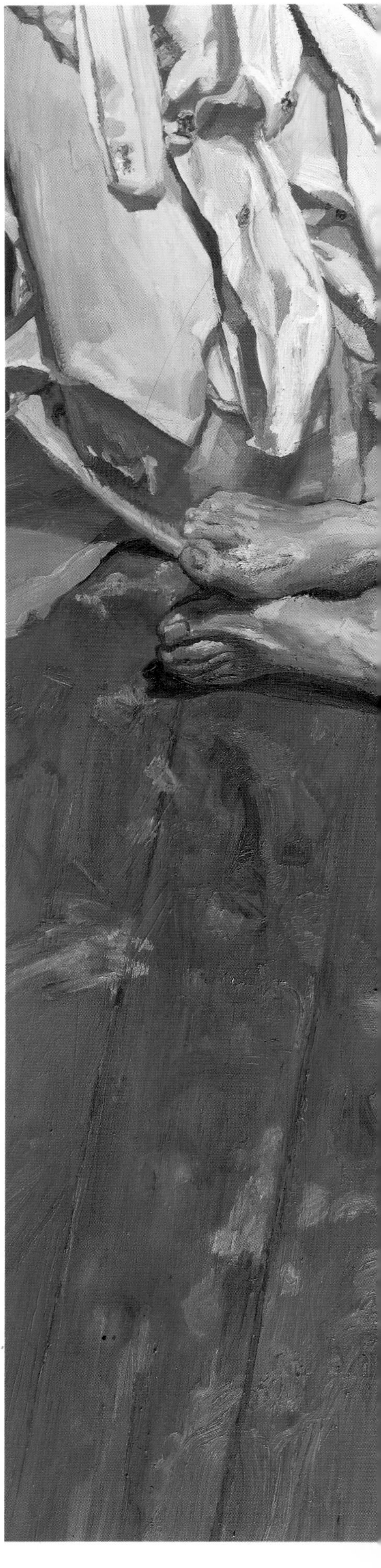

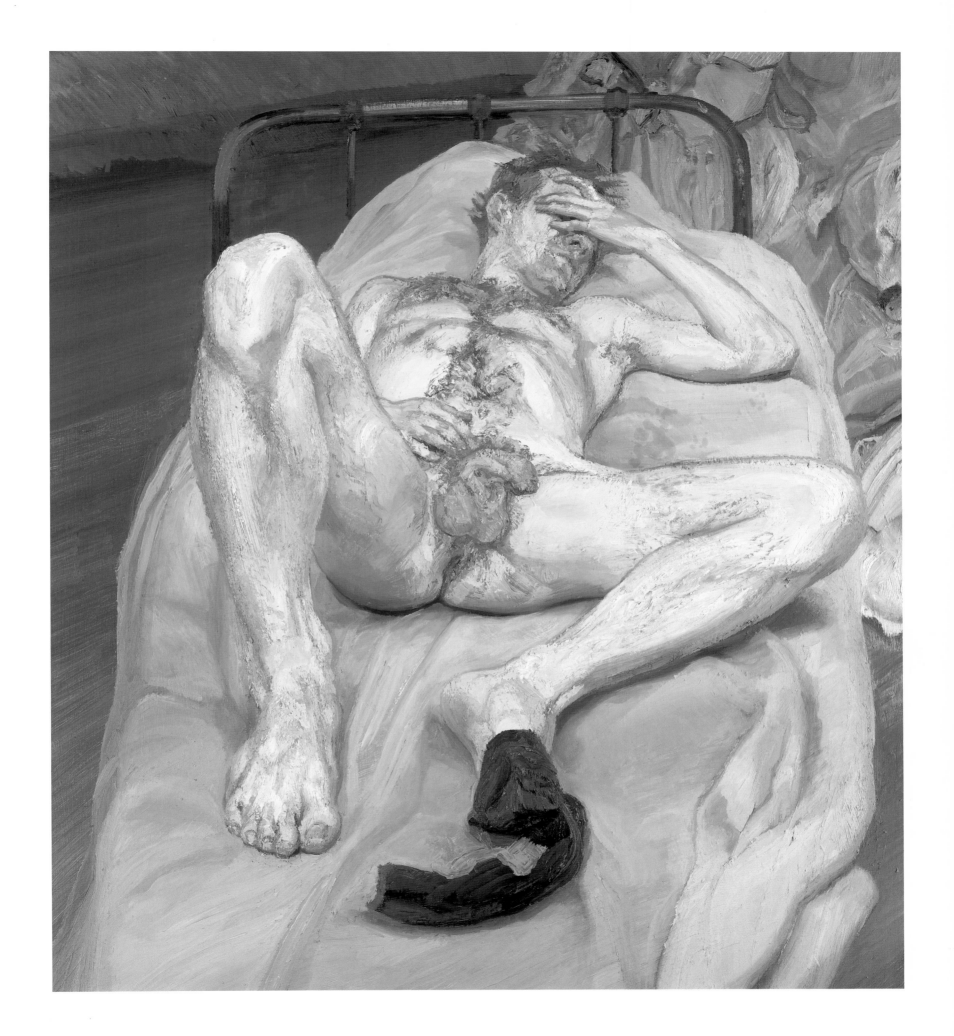

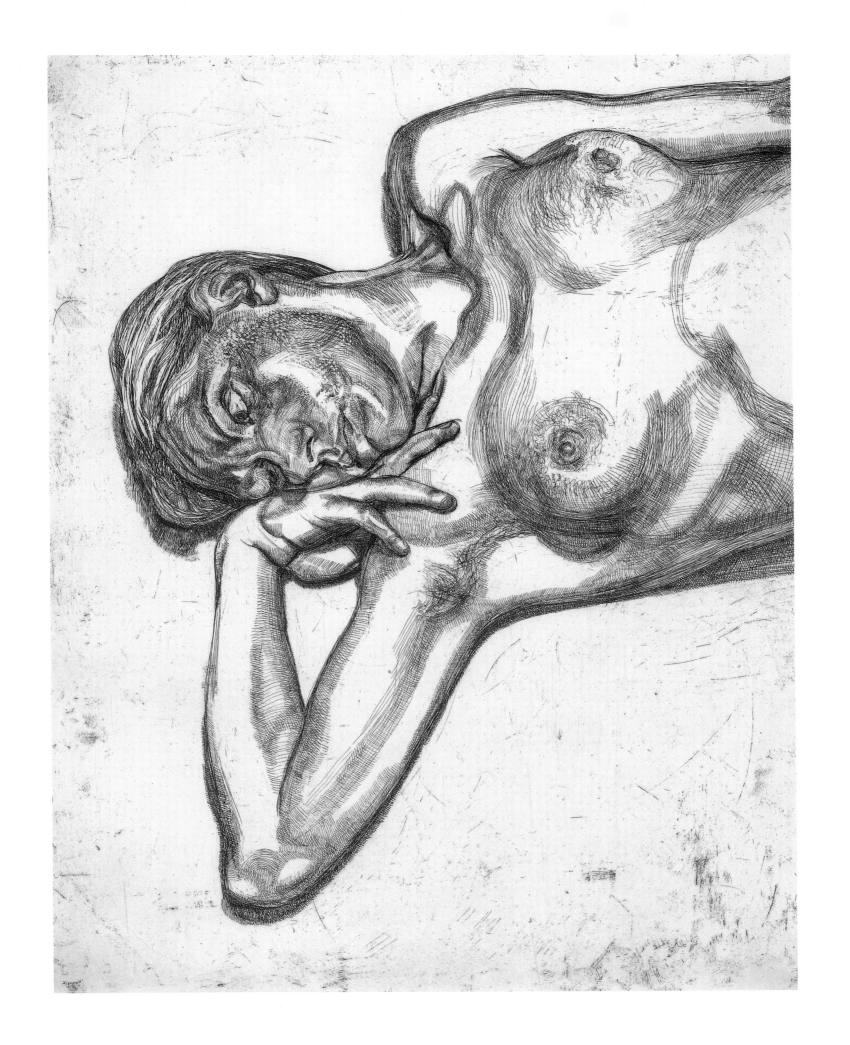

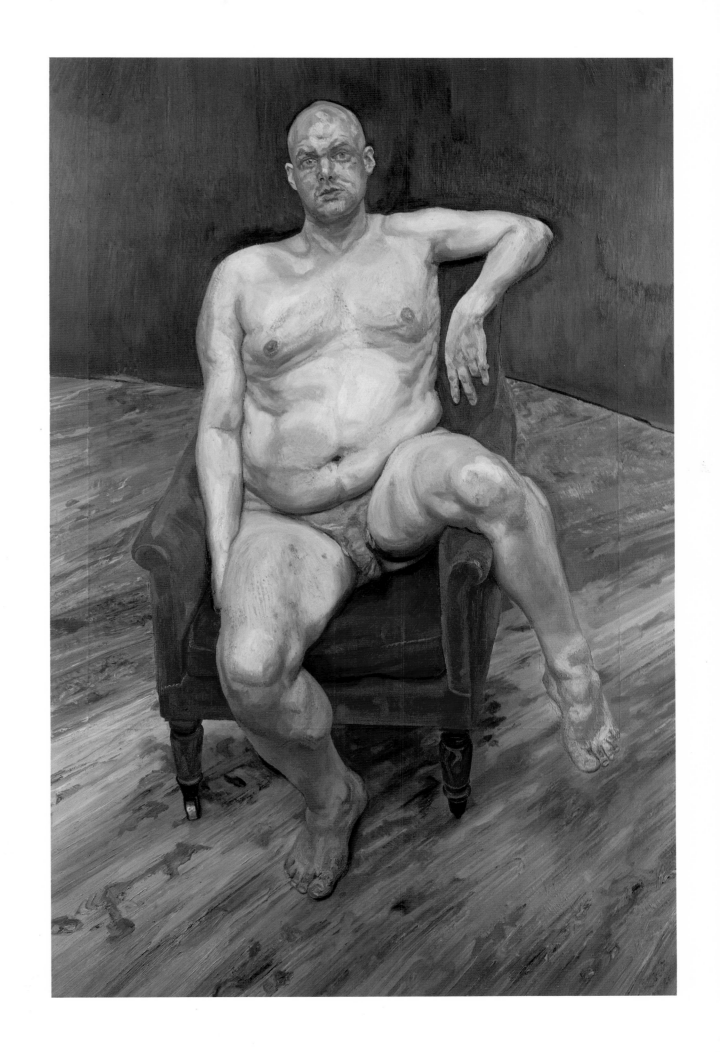

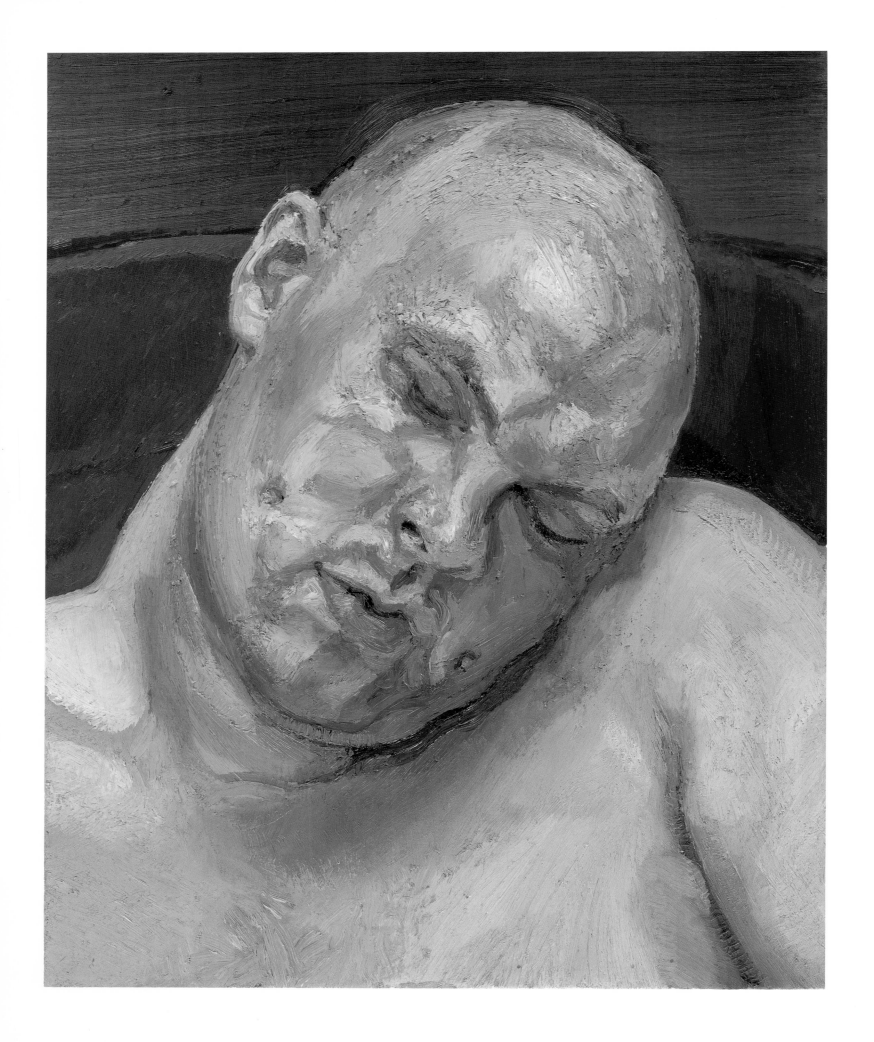

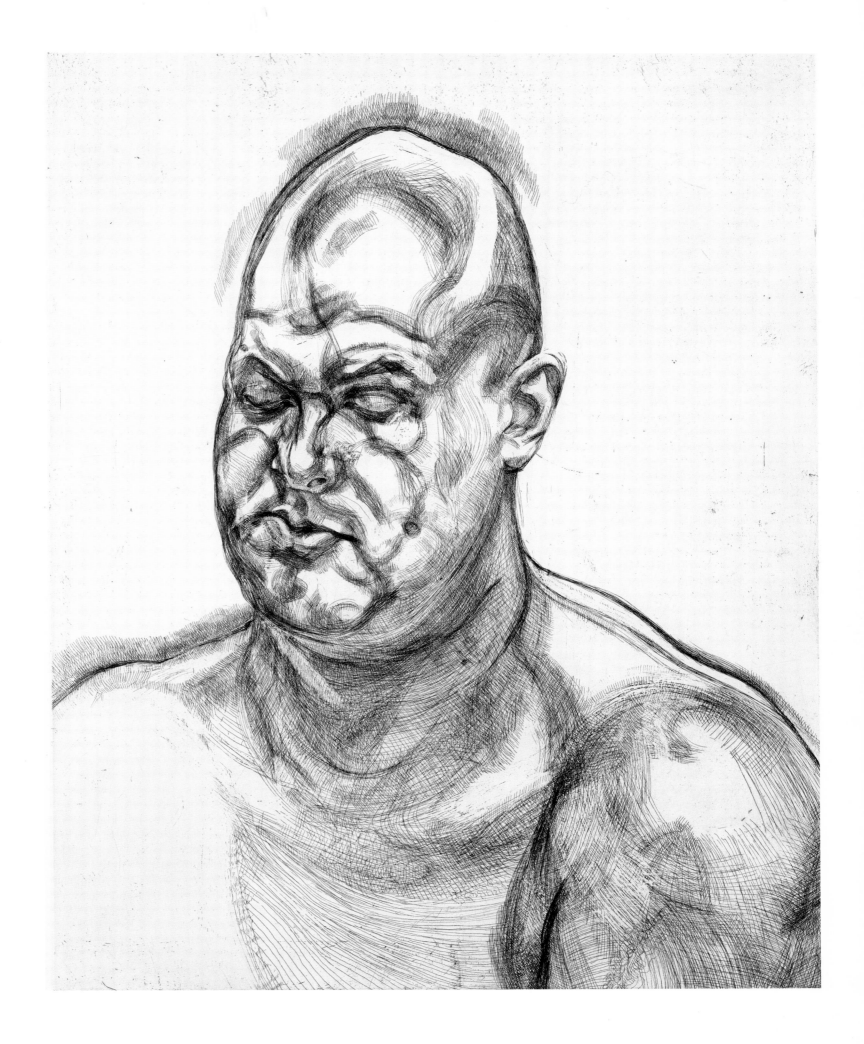

79

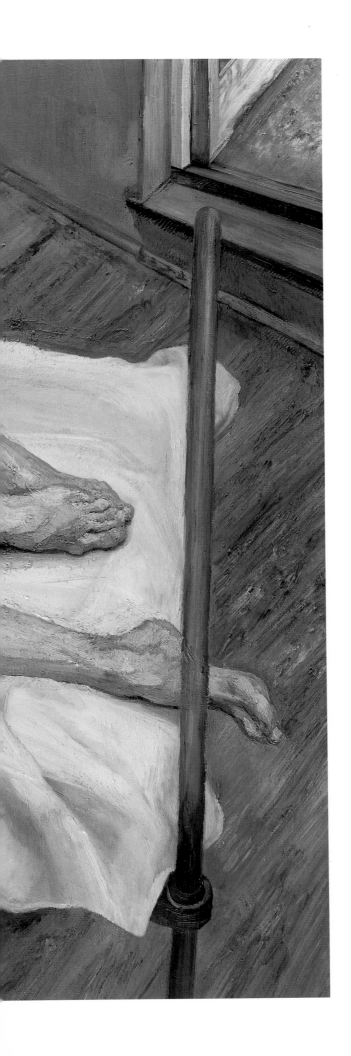

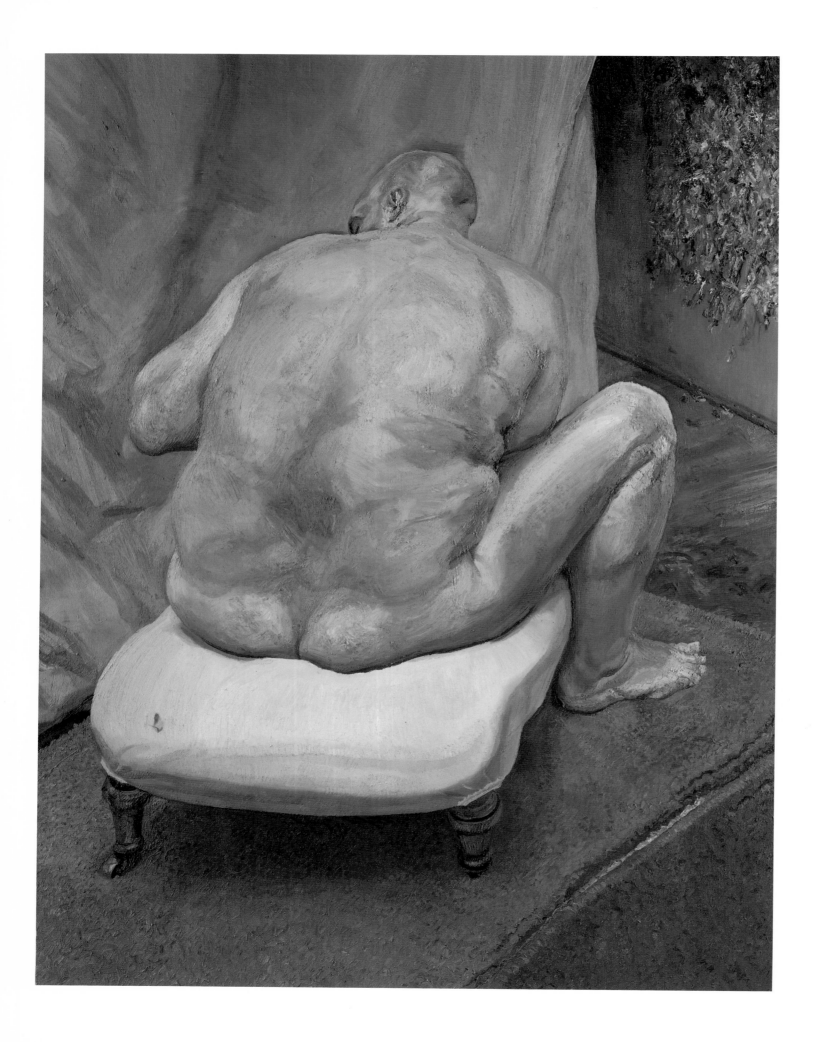

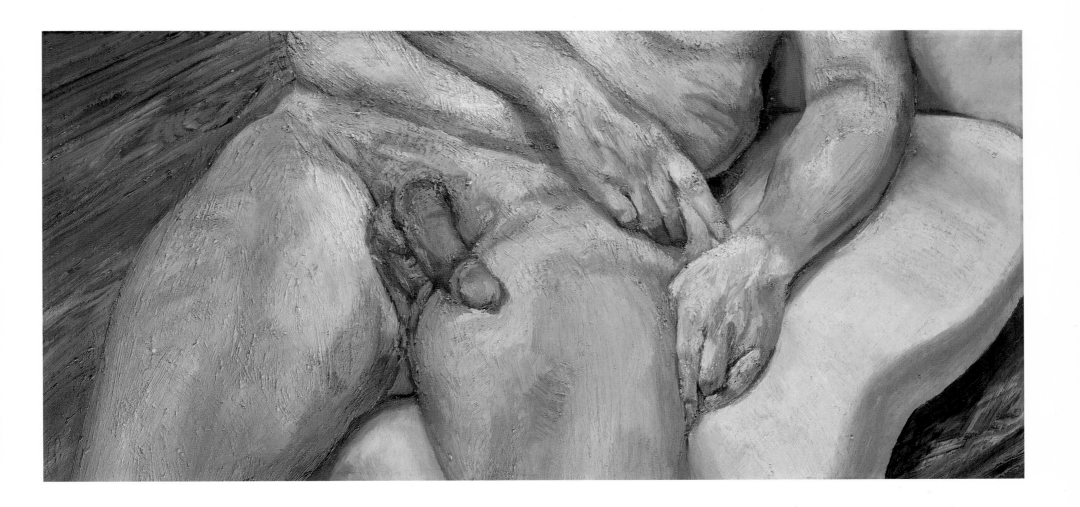

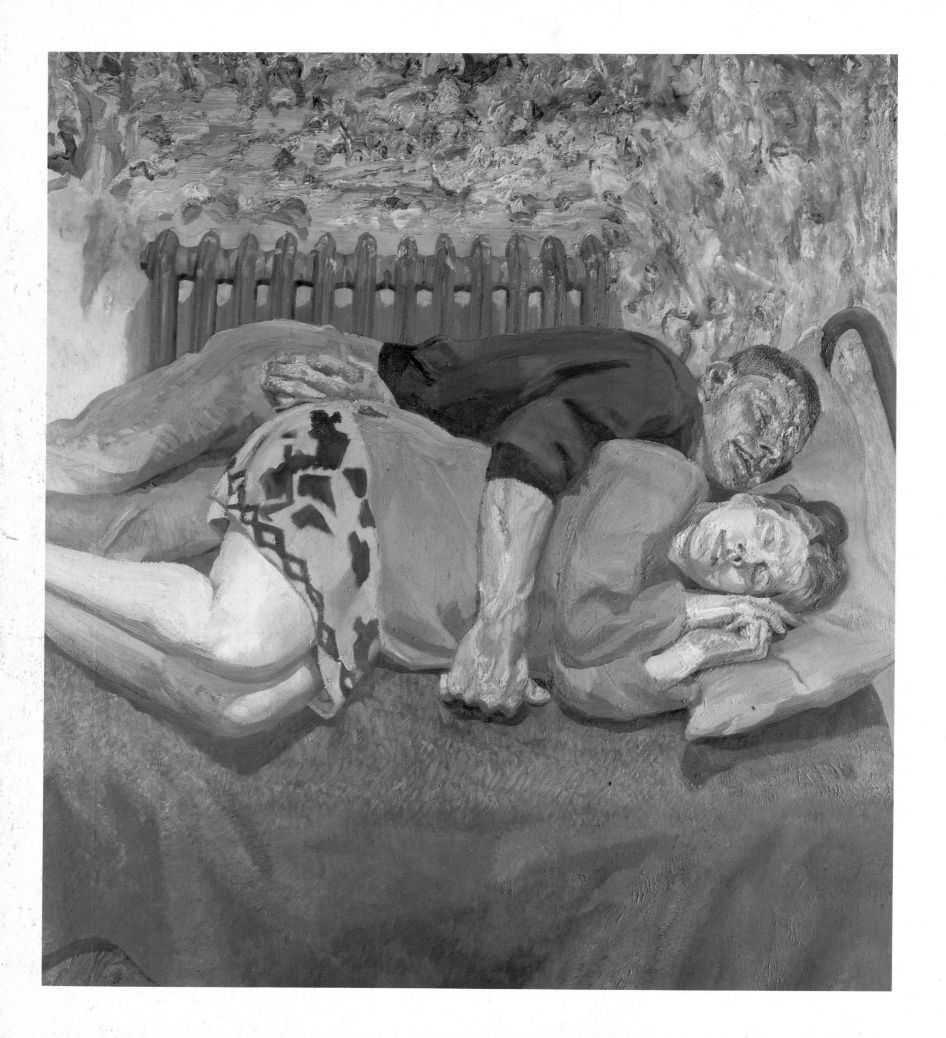

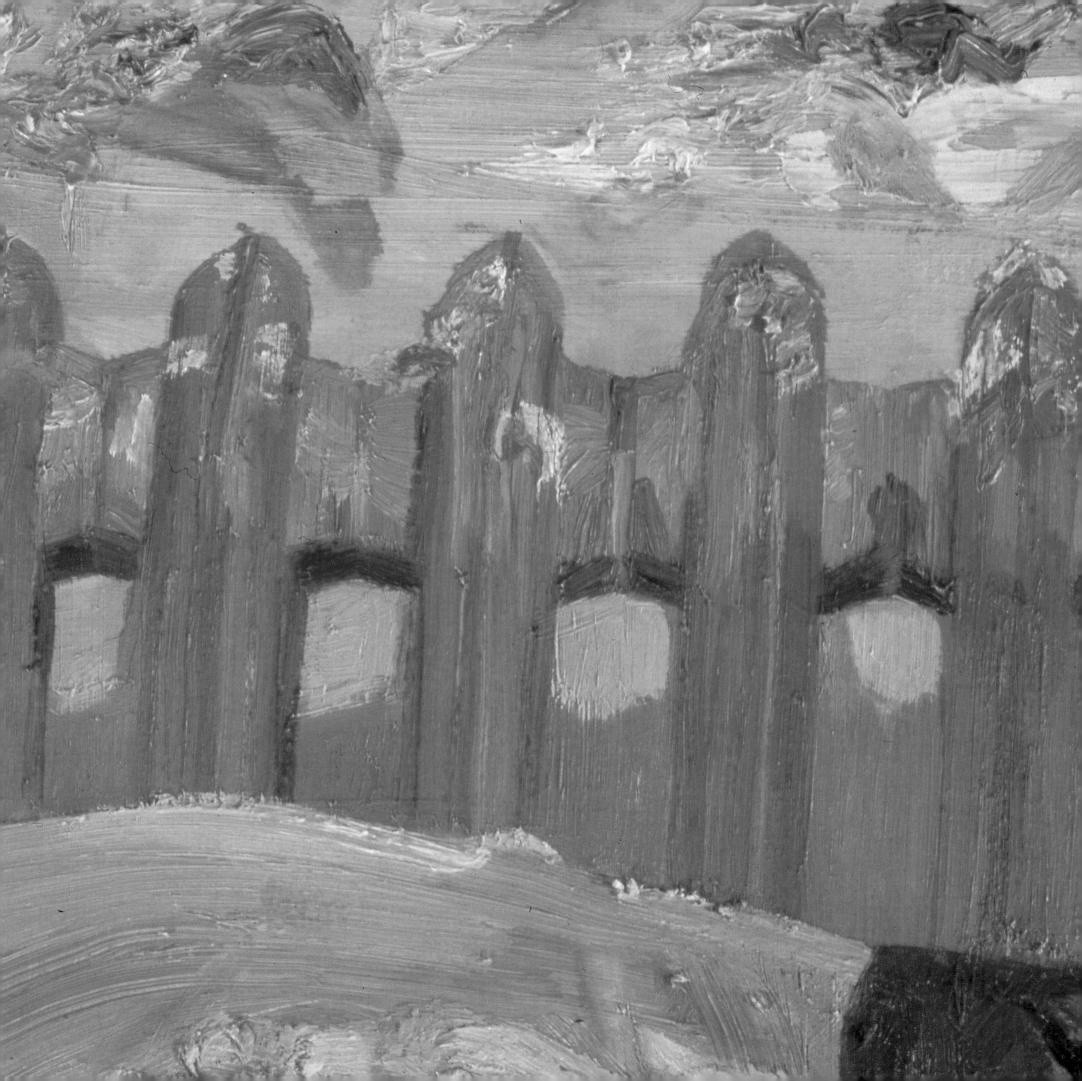

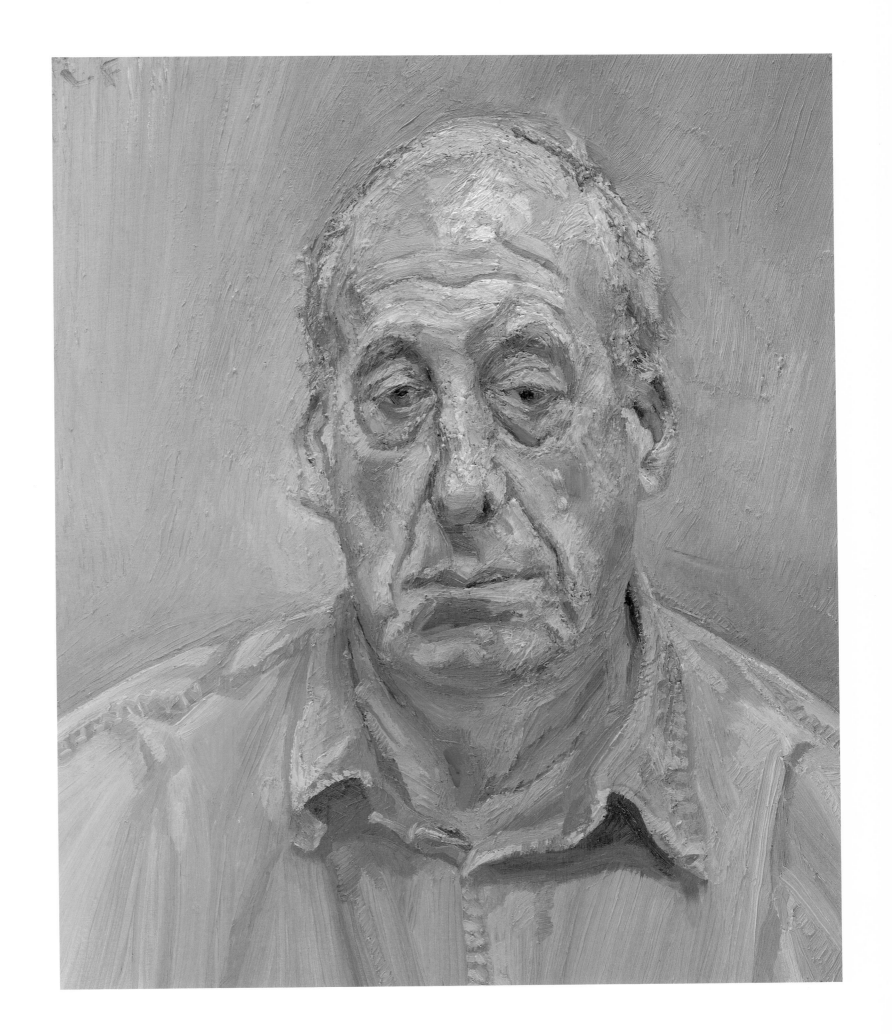

List of Works

Works are shown at all three venues unless indicated otherwise.

1
Woman with a Daffodil
1945
Oil on canvas
9.5 × 5.75 ins/23.75 × 14.25 cm
The Museum of Modern Art, New York. Purchase.
New York only

2
Girl with Roses
1947–48
Oil on canvas
41.5 × 29.25 ins/105.5 × 74.5 cm
The British Council
New York and Madrid only

3
Girl with Leaves
1948
Pastel on grey paper
19 × 16.5 ins/48 × 42 cm
The Museum of Modern Art, New York. Purchase.
New York only

4
Dead Monkey
1950
Pastel and watercolour
8.5 × 14.25 ins/21.25 × 36.25 cm
The Museum of Modern Art, New York. Gift of Lincoln Kirstein.
New York only

5
Interior in Paddington
1951
Oil on canvas
60 × 45 ins/152.5 × 114.25 cm
Board of Trustees of the National Museums and Galleries on Merseyside,
Walker Art Gallery, Liverpool
New York and Madrid only

6
Reflection with Two Children (Self-Portrait)
1965
Oil on canvas
35.75 × 35.75 ins/91 × 91 cm
The Thyssen-Bornemisza Collection, Madrid
New York and Madrid only

7
Naked Girl
1966
Oil on canvas
24 × 24 ins/61 × 61 cm
Steve Martin
New York and Madrid only

8
Interior with Plant, Reflection Listening (Self-Portrait)
1967–68
Oil on canvas
48 × 48 ins/121.75 × 121.75 cm
Private Collection
New York and Madrid only

9
Wasteground with Houses, Paddington
1970–72
Oil on canvas
66 × 40 ins/167.5 × 101.5 cm
Private Collection
New York and Madrid only

10
Two Plants
1977–80
Oil on canvas
60 × 48 ins/152.5 × 122 cm
Tate Gallery, purchased 1980
New York and Madrid only

11
Still Life (Quinces)
1981–82
Oil on canvas
6.25 × 8.25 ins/16 × 21 cm
The Thyssen-Bornemisza Collection
New York and Madrid only

12
Large Interior W11 (after Watteau)
1981–83
Oil on canvas
73 × 78 ins/185.5 × 198.25 cm
Private Collection, Courtesy of James Kirkman Ltd., London
New York and Madrid only

13
The Painter's Mother
1982–84
Oil on canvas
41.5 × 50.25 ins/105.5 × 127.75 cm
Private Collection, Courtesy of James Kirkman Ltd., London

14
Two Irishmen in W11
1984–85
Oil on canvas
68 × 55.75 ins/172.75 × 141.5 cm
Private Collection
New York and Madrid only

15
Lord Goodman
1985
Charcoal
25.25 × 18.75 ins/64.25 × 47.75 cm
Private Collection, Courtesy of James Kirkman Ltd., London

16
Head of Bruce Bernard
1985
Etching
11.75 × 11.75 ins/29.5 × 30 cm (20 × 18.5 ins/51 × 47 cm)
Edition of 50
Published by James Kirkman Ltd., London/Brooke Alexander, New York
Courtesy James Kirkman Ltd., London
London only

17
Girl Holding her Foot
1985
Etching
27.25 × 21.25 ins/69 × 54 cm (35 × 29.5 ins/89 × 75 cm)
Edition of 50
Published by James Kirkman Ltd., London/Brooke Alexander, New York
Courtesy James Kirkman Ltd., London
London only

18
Man Posing
1985–86
Etching
27.5 × 21.5 ins/70 × 54.5 cm (34.75 × 29 ins/88.5 × 74 cm)
Edition of 50
Published by James Kirkman Ltd., London/Brooke Alexander, New York
The Metropolitan Museum of Art, New York
The Elisha Whittelsey Collection
The Elisha Whittelsey Fund, 1988 (1988. 1082)
New York only

19
Night Portrait
1985–86
Oil on canvas
36.5 × 30 ins/92.75 × 76.25 cm
Hirshhorn Museum and Sculpture Garden, Smithsonian
Institution. The Joseph H. Hirshhorn Purchase Fund, 1987

20
Double Portrait
1985–86
Oil on canvas
31 × 35 ins/78.75 × 89 cm
Private Collection

21
Study for Man Smoking
1985
Oil on canvas
24 × 22 ins/61 × 51 cm
Private Collection
London only

22
Man Smoking
1986–87
Oil on canvas
20 × 16 ins/50.75 × 40.75 cm
Private Collection

23
Lord Goodman in his Yellow Pyjamas
1987
Etching with watercolour
12.25 × 16 ins/31 × 40.25 cm (19 × 22.25 ins/48 × 56 cm)
Edition of 50
Published by James Kirkman Ltd., London/Brooke Alexander, New York
Courtesy James Kirkman Ltd., London (for London only)
Courtesy Brooke Alexander, New York (for New York only)

24
Head of a Man
1986
Charcoal
25.25 × 18.75 ins/64.25 × 47.25 cm
The Museum of Modern Art, New York. Gift of Agnes Gund.
New York only

25
Head of a Man
1987
Etching
9 × 7.25 ins/22.5 × 18.25 cm (19.75 × 17.25 ins/50.25 × 44 cm)
Edition of 20
Published by James Kirkman Ltd., London/Brooke Alexander, New York
Courtesy James Kirkman Ltd., London
London only

26
Two Japanese Wrestlers by a Sink
1983–87
Oil on canvas
20 × 31 ins/51 × 78.75 cm
The Art Institute of Chicago
Restricted gift of Mrs Frederic G. Pick;
through prior gift of Mr and Mrs Carter H. Harrison, 1987.275
New York and Madrid only

27
Naked Man on a Bed
1987
Oil on canvas
22.25 × 24 ins/56.5 × 61 cm
Saatchi Collection, London

28
Naked Man on a Bed
1987
Etching
14.5 × 20.5 ins/37 × 52 cm (22.5 × 29.25 ins/57.25 × 74.5 cm)
Edition of 10
Published by James Kirkman Ltd., London/Brooke Alexander, New York
Courtesy James Kirkman Ltd., London
London only

29
Blond Girl on a Bed
1987
Oil on canvas
16.25 × 20 ins/41 × 51 cm
Saatchi Collection, London

30
Girl Sitting
1987
Etching
21 × 27.75 ins/53 × 70.5 cm (27 × 32.25 ins/68.5 × 82 cms)
Edition of 50
Published by James Kirkman Ltd., London/Brooke Alexander, New York
Private Collection
London only

31
Girl Sitting
1987–88
Oil on canvas
21.5 × 22 ins/54.5 × 55.75 cm
Saatchi Collection, London

32
Two Men
1987–88
Oil on canvas
42 × 29.5 ins/106.75 × 75 cm
Scottish National Gallery of Modern Art, Edinburgh
London and New York only

33
Naked Woman
1988
Oil on canvas
27.75 × 31.75 ins/70.5 × 80.5 cm
The Saint Louis Art Museum: Museum Purchase:
Funds given by Dr. and Mrs Alvin Frank, Mr and Mrs Lester A. Crnacer, Jr.,
Mr and Mrs George Schlapp, and The Siteman Contemporary Art Fund
London and New York only

34
Bella and Esther
1988
Oil on canvas
29 × 35 ins/73.75 × 89 cm
Private Collection

35
Annabel Sleeping
1987–88
Oil on canvas
22 × 15.25 ins/56 × 38.75 cm
Private Collection, London

36
Triple Portrait
1987–88
Oil on canvas
8.5 × 10 ins/21.5 × 25.5 cm
Private Collection

37
Cerith
1988
Oil on canvas
9.5 × 6.5 ins/24.25 × 16.25 cm
Private Collection

38
Susie
1988
Oil on canvas
10.75 × 8.75 ins/27.25 × 22.25 cm
James Kirkman Ltd., London/Robert Miller Gallery, New York

39
Woman in a Grey Sweater
1988
Oil on canvas
22 × 18 ins/56 × 45.75 cm
Saatchi Collection, London

40
Man Resting
1988
Oil on canvas
9.5 × 13 ins/24.25 × 33.25 cm
Private Collection

41
Frances Glory
1988
Oil on canvas
6.5 × 9.5 ins/16.25 × 24.25 cm
Private Collection

42
Man's Head and Arm
1988
Oil on canvas
9.5 × 6.5 ins/24.25 × 16.5 cm
Collection Jasper Johns

43
Pluto
1988
Etching, drypoint and watercolour
12.5 × 23.75 ins/32 × 60 cm (16.5 × 27 ins/42 × 68.5 cm)
Edition of 40
Published by James Kirkman Ltd., London/Brooke Alexander, New York
Courtesy James Kirkman Ltd., London (for London only)
Courtesy Brooke Alexander, New York (for New York only)

44
Man Resting
1988
Etching
14.5 × 16.25 ins/37 × 41 cm (18.5 × 19.75 ins/47 × 50.25 cm)
Edition of 30
Published by James Kirkman Ltd., London/Brooke Alexander, New York
Courtesy James Kirkman Ltd., London (for London only)
Courtesy Brooke Alexander, New York (for New York only)

45
Head of Ib
1988
Etching
8.25 × 5.75 ins/21 × 14.5 cm (14.25 × 11 ins/36.25 × 28 cm)
Edition of 40
Published by James Kirkman Ltd., London/Brooke Alexander, New York
Courtesy James Kirkman Ltd., London
London only

46
Cerith
1989
Pastel over etching
13.75 × 10.25 ins/35 × 26 cm
Collection PaineWebber Group Inc., New York
Not in exhibition

47
Two Men in the Studio
1987–89
Oil on canvas
73 × 47.5 ins/185.5 × 120.75 cm
Saatchi Collection, London

48
Two Men in the Studio
1989
Etching
9 × 8 ins/23 × 20.25 cm (16 × 14.25 ins/40.75 × 36.25 cm)
Edition of 25
Published by James Kirkman Ltd., London/Brooke Alexander, New York
Courtesy James Kirkman Ltd., London
London only

49
Standing by the Rags
1988–89
Oil on canvas
66.25 × 54.5 ins/168.25 × 138.5 cm
Tate Gallery, purchased with assistance from the National Art Collections Fund, the Friends of the Tate Gallery and anonymous donors, 1990

50
Susie
1988–89
Oil on canvas
20.5 × 22.25 ins/52 × 56.5 cm
Courtesy Thomas Gibson Fine Art Ltd.
London and New York only

51
Pluto
1989
Charcoal
30 × 22.5 ins/76.25 × 57.25 cm
The Art Institute of Chicago
Through prior gift of Mrs Gilbert Chapman in memory of Charles B.
Goodspeed; through prior bequest of Maxine Kunstadter, 1989. 474
London and New York only

52
The Painter's Mother Dead
1989
Charcoal
13 × 9.5 ins/33.25 × 24.5 cm
The Cleveland Museum of Art, Delia E. Holden Fund 89. 100
London and New York only

53
Man in a String Chair
1988–89
Oil on canvas
59 × 40.25 ins/150 × 102 cm
Private Collection

54
Man in a Chair
1989
Oil on canvas
45.25 × 31.5 ins/115 × 80 cm
Private Collection

55
Chris Bramham
1989
Oil on canvas
12.5 × 10.75 ins/31.75 × 27.25 cm
Private Collection

56
Head of a Woman
1988–90
Oil on canvas
13.5 × 9.5 ins/34.25 × 24.25 cm
Private Collection, USA

57
Naked Man on a Bed
1989
Oil on canvas
13.75 × 10.25 ins/35 × 26 cm
Private Collection

58
Lying by the Rags
1989–90
Oil on canvas
54.5 × 72.5 ins/138.5 x184.25 cm
Private Collection

59
Naked Man on a Bed
1989–90
Oil on canvas
32 × 27.25 ins/81.25 × 69.25 cm
James Kirkman Ltd., London/Robert Miller Gallery, New York

60
Annabel
1990
Oil on canvas
9.5 × 6.5 ins/24.25 × 16.5 cm
Private Collection

61
Head and Shoulders of a Girl
1990
Etching
27.5 × 21.5 ins/69.5 × 54.5 cm (30.75 × 24.75 ins/78 × 63.25 cm)
Edition of 50
Published by James Kirkman Ltd., London/Brooke Alexander, New York
The Metropolitan Museum of Art, New York
Purchase, Anonymous Gift, 1991 (1991. 102)
New York only

62
Susie
1989–90
Oil on canvas
12 × 12 ins/30.75 × 30.75 cm
Hal and Jesse Kant

63
Ib
1990
Oil on canvas
11 × 10 ins/28 × 25.5 cm
James Kirkman Ltd., London/Robert Miller Gallery, New York

64
Head of a Woman
1990–91
Oil on canvas
15 × 12 ins/38 × 30.5 cm
Private Collection

65
Self Portrait
1990–91
Oil on canvas
12 × 12 ins/30.5 × 30.5cm
Collection of Mr and Mrs S.I. Newhouse, Jr.
New York only

66
Leigh Bowery (Seated)
1990
Oil on canvas
96 × 72 ins/243.75 × 183 cm
Mr. and Mrs. Richard C. Hedreen

67
Naked Portrait on a Red Sofa
1989–91
Oil on canvas
39.5 × 35.5 ins/100.25 × 90.25 cm
Private Collection

68
Woman in a Butterfly Jersey
1990–91
Oil on canvas
39.5 × 32 ins/100.25 × 81.25 cm
Private Collection

69
Seated Nude
1990–91
Oil on canvas
18 × 20 ins/45.75 × 50.75 cm
James Kirkman Ltd., London/Thomas Gibson Fine Art Ltd., London

70
Polly, Barney and Christopher Bramham
1990–91
Oil on canvas
28.25 × 32 ins/72 × 81.5 cm
James Kirkman Ltd., London/Robert Miller Gallery, New York

71
Head of a Man
1991
Oil on canvas
24 × 17.75 ins/61 × 45 cm
Private Collection

72
Head of a Man
1991
Oil on canvas
20 × 16 ins/50.75 × 40.5 cm
Private Collection

73
Nude with Leg Up
1992
Oil on canvas
72 × 90 ins/183 × 229 cm
Hirshhorn Museum and Sculpture Garden, Smithsonian Institution

74
Leigh Bowery
1991
Oil on canvas
20 × 16 ins/50.75 × 40.5 cm
Private Collection

75
Large Head
1993
Etching
27.25 × 21.25 ins/59.5 × 54.5 cm (32.5 × 26.25 ins/82.5 × 66.75 cm)
Edition of 40
Published by Matthew Marks Gallery, New York
Courtesy Matthew Marks Gallery, New York
London only

76
Esther
1991
Etching
8.75 × 8 ins/22 × 20.25 cm (17.25 × 15.5 ins/44 × 39.25 cm)
Edition of 25
Published by James Kirkman Ltd., London/Brooke Alexander, New York
Courtesy James Kirkman Ltd., London
London only

77
Head of Esther
1992
Oil on canvas
24 × 20.25 ins/61 × 51.5 cm
Private Collection

78
Landscape
1993
Etching
5.75 × 7.75 ins/15 × 19.75 cm (14 × 15.25 ins/35.5 × 38.75 cm)
Edition of 30
Published by Matthew Marks Gallery, New York
Courtesy Matthew Marks Gallery, New York
London only

79
Still Life with Book
1991–92
Oil on canvas
7.5 × 9.5 ins/19 × 24.25 cm
Private Collection, Mexico City

80
Bruce Bernard
1992
Oil on canvas
45 × 33 ins/114.25 × 83.75 cm
Private Collection

81
Two Women
1992
Oil on canvas
60.25 × 84.5 ins/153 × 214.75 cm
Private Collection, USA

82
Woman Holding her Thumb
1992
Oil on canvas
52 × 48 ins/132 × 122 cm
Acquavella Contemporary Art Inc., New York

83
Kai
1991–92
Oil on canvas
24.5 × 20.25 ins/62.25 × 51.5 cm
Private Collection

84
Kai
1991–92
Etching
27.25 × 21.25 ins/59.5 × 54.5 cm (31.25 × 25 ins/79.25 × 63.5 cm)
Edition of 40
Published by Matthew Marks Gallery, New York
/James Kirkman Ltd., London
London only

85
Naked Man, Back View
1991–92
Oil on canvas
72 × 54 ins/183 × 137.25 cm
The Metropolitan Museum of Art, New York
Purchase, Lila Acheson Wallace Gift, 1993 (1993.71)

86
Parts of Leigh Bowery
1992
Oil on canvas
19.5 × 41 ins/49.5 × 104.25 cm
Private Collection
London and Madrid only

87
Ib and her Husband
1992
Oil on canvas
66.25 × 57.75 ins/168 × 147 cm
Private Collection

88
And the Bridegroom
1993
Oil on canvas
91.25 × 77.25 ins/232 × 196 cm
Private Collection

89
Portrait of Francis Wyndham
1993
Oil on canvas
25.25 × 20.5 ins/64 × 52 cm
Private Collection

90
Still Life with Book
1993
Oil on canvas
18 × 20 ins/45.75 × 51 cm
Private Collection

91
Painter Working, Reflection (frontispiece: work in progress)
1993
Oil on canvas
40 × 32.25 ins/101.25 × 81.75cm
Private Collection

Chronology

Born 8 December 1922 in Berlin, son of Lucie Brasch and Ernst Freud. His mother was the daughter of a grain merchant and Ernst, Sigmund Freud's youngest son, was an architect. The family lived near the Tiergarten and spent summers at Hiddensee near Rügen on the Baltic and on Freud's maternal grandfather's estate near Kotbus. In 1933 the family moved to England and in 1939 Freud became a naturalized British subject. Together with his brothers, Stefan and Clemens, he began boarding at Dartington Hall school, later moving to Bryanston. In Autumn 1938 Freud enrolled at the Central School of Arts and Crafts. The following year he began working at the East Anglian School of Drawing and Painting at Dedham, run by Cedric Morris, and spent most of his time there until April 1941 when he signed on a vessel in the Merchant Navy, staying three months, and returning occasionally to the school which had moved to Hadleigh in Suffolk. In 1939 and 1943 Freud's work was published in *Horizon* magazine and a room of his paintings was hung at the Lefèvre Gallery in 1944. Freud spent the Autumn of 1946 in Paris and then travelled on to Greece. In 1948 he married Kitty Garman, daughter of Jacob Epstein, and in 1952 married Caroline Blackwood. He rented a flat in Delamere Terrace in 1943 and stayed in that area of Paddington for the next thirty years before moving to Holland Park. In 1951 he won an Arts Council purchase prize for his contribution to the Festival of Britain. He was a visiting tutor at the Slade from 1949 to 1954 and on odd occasions in later years. Lawrence Gowing wrote a monograph published by Thames and Hudson in 1982. He is represented by Acquavella Contemporary Art Inc. in New York.

Selected One Person Exhibitions

1944
Lefèvre Gallery, London

1946
Lefèvre Gallery, London (with Ben Nicholson, Graham Sutherland, Francis Bacon, Robert Colquhoun, John Craxton, Robert MacBryde and Julian Trevelyan)

1947
The London Gallery

1948
The London Gallery (with James Gleeson, Robert Klippel, John Pemberton, Cawthra Mulock)

1950
Hanover Gallery, London

1952
Hanover Gallery, London

1954
British Pavilion XXVII Venice Biennale (the other artists in the British contribution were Ben Nicholson and Francis Bacon)

1958
Marlborough Fine Art, London

1963
Marlborough Fine Art, London

1968
Marlborough Fine Art, London

1972
Anthony d'Offay, London
Gray Art Gallery, Hartlepool

1974
Retrospective exhibition, organised by the Arts Council of Great Britain, catalogue by John Russell: Hayward Gallery, London; Bristol City Art Gallery; Birmingham City Museum and Art Gallery; Leeds City Museum and Art Gallery; 'Pages from a sketchbook of 1941', Anthony d'Offay, London

1978
Anthony d'Offay, London

1979
Davis & Long Co., New York; Nishimura Gallery, Tokyo, catalogue by Seiji Oshima

1982
Anthony d'Offay, London

1983
Thomas Agnew & Sons, London; Bernard Jacobson, London (etchings)

1984
Rex Irwin Gallery, Sydney (with Frank Auerbach, Francis Bacon and Leon Kossoff); 'Lucian Freud, A Painting and Etchings', Nishimura Gallery, Tokyo

1987–88
'Lucian Freud Paintings', catalogue by Robert Hughes, reprinted by Thames & Hudson. Retrospective exhibition organised by The British Council: Hirshhorn Museum and Sculpture Garden, Smithsonian Institution, Washington DC; Musée National d'Art Moderne, Paris; Hayward Gallery, South Bank Centre, London with an added section of new paintings and prints; Neue Nationalgalerie Berlin.

1988
'Lucian Freud Etchings, 1982–88', Rex Irwin Gallery, Sydney

1988–89
'Lucian Freud, Works on Paper', catalogue by Nicholas Penny and Robert Flynn Johnson, organised by The South Bank Centre: Ashmolean Museum, Oxford; The Fruitmarket Gallery, Edinburgh; Ferens Art Gallery, Hull; Walker Art Gallery, Liverpool; Royal Albert Memorial Museum, Exeter; The Fine Arts Museums of San Francisco, California Palace of the Legion of Honor, San Francisco; Minneapolis Institute of Art; Brooke Alexander Gallery, New York; Cleveland Museum of Art, Ohio; The Saint Louis Art Museum, Missouri

1989
'Lucian Freud, Paintings 1947–1987', Scottish National Gallery of Modern Art, Edinburgh; 'Lucian Freud, Early Works', the Fruitmarket Gallery, Edinburgh

1990
'Lucian Freud, l'oeuvre gravé', catalogue by Michael Peppiatt, Galerie Berggruen, Paris; Saatchi Collection, London (with Frank Auerbach and Richard Deacon)

1991
'Lucian Freud, Etchings 1946–90', Nishimura Gallery, Tokyo; 'Lucian Freud, The Complete Etchings 1946–1991', Thomas Gibson, London, catalogue by Craig Hartley

1991–92
'Lucian Freud, Paintings and Works on Paper 1940–1991', catalogue by Bruno Mantura and Angus Cook, organised by The British Council: Palazzo Ruspoli, Rome; Castello Sforzesca, Milan; Tate Gallery, Liverpool; Tochigi Prefectural Museum of Fine Arts; Otani Memorial Museum, Nishinomiya; Setagaya Art Museum, Tokyo

1992–93
'Lucian Freud', catalogue by William Feaver, organised by The British Council: Art Gallery of New South Wales, Sydney; Art Gallery of Western Australia, Perth

Selected Mixed Exhibitions

1942
New Year Exhibition, Leicester Gallery, London

1948
'Forty Years of Modern Art', Institute of Contemporary Art, London; 'Exposition de la jeune peinture en Bretagne', Galerie René Drouin, Paris

1950
'London–Paris', Institute of Contemporary Art, New Burlington Galleries, London

1951
'21 Modern British Painters', The British Council, Vancouver; 'Sixty Paintings for '51', the Arts Council of Great Britain, London, for the Festival of Britain; 'British Paintings 1925–50', the Arts Council of Great Britain, London

1952
'Recent Trends in Realist Painting', Institute of Contemporary Art, London

1953
'Portraits by Contemporary British Artists', Marlborough Fine Art, London

1955
'Daily Express Young Artists' Exhibition',
New Burlington Galleries, London

1960–61
'Modern British Portraits', the Arts Council of Great
Britain tour

1962
'British Self Portraits from Sickert to the Present Day',
the Arts Council of Great Britain, London

1963
The Dunn International and Exhibition of
Contemporary Painting, Beaverbrook Art Gallery,
Fredericton, New Brunswick and Tate Gallery, London

1967
'English Paintings 1951–1967', Norwich Castle
Museum

1970
'Zeitgenossen', Städtische Kunsthalle, Recklinghausen

1971
'Snap', National Portrait Gallery, London

1974–75
'La ricerca dell'identità', Palazzo Reale, Milan

1975
'English Portraits', National Museum of Western Art,
Tokyo; 'The Nude', Morley Gallery, London; 'Drawings
of People', the Arts Council of Great Britain tour;
'British Exhibition, Art 6 '75', Schweizer
Münstermesse, Basel

1975–76
'European Paintings in the Seventies, new work by
sixteen Artists', Los Angeles County Museum of Art;
St Louis Art Museum; Elvejhem Art Center

1976
'The Human Clay', the Arts Council of Great Britain,
Hayward Gallery, London; 'Real Life', Peter Moores's
Liverpool Project 4, Walker Art Gallery, Liverpool

1979
'The British Art Show', the Arts Council of Great
Britain touring exhibition

1979–80
'Treasures from Chatsworth: The Devonshire
Inheritance', Royal Academy of Arts, London; Virginia
Museum of Fine Arts, Richmond, Virginia; Kimbell
Art Museum, Fort Worth, Texas; The Toledo Museum
of Art, Toledo, Ohio; San Antonio Museum Association,
San Antonio, Texas; New Orleans Museum of Art, New
Orleans, Louisiana; The Fine Arts Museums of San
Francisco, California Palace of the Legion of Honor,
San Francisco

1981
'Eight Figurative Artists', catalogue by Lawrence
Gowing, Yale Center for British Art, New Haven;
Santa Barbara Museum of Art, Santa Barbara;
'A New Spirit in Painting', Royal Academy
of Arts, London

1982
'Aspects of British Art Today', Tokyo Metropolitan Art
Museum; Tochigi Prefectural Museum of Fine Arts;
The National Museum of Fine Arts, Osaka; Fukuoka
Art Museum; Hokkaido Museum of Modern Art

1984
'The Hard-Won Image', catalogue by Richard
Morphet, Tate Gallery, London; 'As of Now', Peter
Moores's Project 7, Walker Art Gallery, Liverpool;
'Creation: The Natural History of Modern Art', Scottish
National Gallery of Modern Art, Edinburgh, 'Capital
Painting, Pictures from Corporate Collections in the
City of London', Barbican Art Gallery, London

1984–85
'The Proper Study', catalogue by William Feaver,
organised by The British Council: Lalit Kala Akademi,
Delhi; Jehangir Nicholson Museum of Modern Art,
Bombay

1985
'The British Show', catalogue by John McEwen,
organised by The British Council: Art Gallery of
Western Australia, Perth; Art Gallery of New South
Wales, Sydney; Queensland Art Gallery, Brisbane;
'A Singular Vision', Royal Albert Memorial Museum,
Exeter; Milton Keynes Exhibition Gallery; Atkinson
Art Gallery, Southport, Merseyside; Laing Art Gallery,
Newcastle-upon-Tyne; Cooper Gallery, Barnsley; South
London Art Gallery, Peckham, London

1985–86
'Carnegie International', Museum of Art, Carnegie Institute, Pittsburgh

1986
'Forty Years of Modern Art', Tate Gallery, London; 'Art and Model', Whitworth Art Gallery, University of Manchester

1986–87
'Contrariwise, Surrealism and Britain 1930–36', Swansea Festival Exhibition, Glynn Vivian Art Gallery, Swansea; Victoria Art Gallery, Bath; Polytechnic Gallery, Newcastle; Mostyn Art Gallery, Llandudno

1987
'British Art in the 20th Century', Royal Academy of Arts, London; 'A Paradise Lost', Barbican Art Gallery, London; 'The Artist's Eye', National Gallery, London; 'Englische Kunst im 20 Jahrhundert', Staatsgalerie, Stuttgart

1987–88
'A School of London: Six Figurative Painters', catalogue by Michael Peppiatt, Kunstnernes Hus, Oslo; Museum of Modern Art, Louisiana; Museo d'Arte Moderna, Ca'Pesaro, Venice; Kunstmuseum, Düsseldorf; 'L'Art en Europe, 1945–56': Musée d'Art Moderne, Sainte Etienne

1988
'The Magic Mirror', Scottish National Gallery of Modern Art, Edinburgh; 'The Face', Arkansas Art Center, Little Rock, Arkansas

1989
'Monet to Freud', Sotheby's, London

1990
'The Pursuit of the Real: British Figurative Painting from Sickert to Bacon', catalogue by Tim Wilcox, Andrew Causey & Lynda Checketts, Manchester City Art Galleries, Manchester; Barbican Art Gallery, London; Glasgow City Art Gallery, Glasgow; 'The British Imagination, Twentieth Century Paintings, Sculpture and Drawings', Hirschl & Adler Galleries, New York; 'Avant-garde British Printmaking', The British Museum, London; 'Masterpieces from the Arts Council Collection', Ueno Royal Museum, Tokyo; 'Festival of Fifty-one', Royal Festival Hall, London; 'Glasgow's Great British Art Exhibition', McLellan Galleries, Glasgow

1990–91
'For a Wider World: Sixty works in the British Council Collection', Ukranian Museum of Fine Arts, Kiev; Musée National d'Histoire et d'Art Luxembourg; SS Cyril and Methodius International Foundation, Sofia; Museo de Bellas Artes, Buenos Aires

1991
'Like the Face of the Moon', South Bank Centre; Bolton Museum and Art Gallery; Stoke-on-Trent City Museum and Art Gallery; Mead Gallery, University of Warwick, Coventry; Glynn Vivian Art Gallery, Swansea; 'Art of the Forties', Museum of Modern Art, New York; 'In Human Terms', Stiebel Modern, New York

1991–92
'Da Bacon a Oggi. The Outsider in British Figuration', Palazzo Vecchio, Florence

Statements by the Artist

1954
'Lucian Freud, some thoughts on painting', *Encounter*, July

1963
'Lucian Freud, a short text', *Cambridge Opinion*, 37

1985
'Lucian Freud', 'Carnegie International', Museum of Art, Carnegie Institute, Pittsburgh, p.131

1987
'Lucian Freud, the Artist's Eye', The National Gallery, London, June-August

Monograph

1982
Gowing, Lawrence, 'Lucian Freud', Thames and Hudson, London

The British Council's Australian Catalogue (1992–93) contains a complete bibliography.

The Whitechapel Art Gallery opened in 1901 and is administered by a charitable trust. The trust has no endowment and the Gallery's existence and programme therefore depend wholly on financial assistance given by national and local authorities, companies (through sponsorship and donations), foundations, trusts and individuals. In 1984, the Whitechapel Art Gallery Foundation was established to stimulate support from the business community and charitable sector.

The Whitechapel gratefully acknowledges the financial assistance which it has been receiving from:

Arts Council of Great Britain
Foundation for Sport and the Arts
London Arts Board
London Docklands Development Corporation
London Borough of Tower Hamlets
London Boroughs Grants Scheme
Ministry of Foreign Affairs, Spain
Visiting Arts

We would also like to acknowledge the generous assistance of:

Foundations and Trusts

Aldgate and Allhallows Barking Exhibition Foundation
The Baring Foundation
The Clore Foundation
The David Cohen Family Charitable Trust
Drapers' Hall
Edwin C. Cohen and the Echoing Green Foundation
Esmee Fairbairn Charitable Trust
The Ruth and Stuart Lipton Charitable Trust
The Henry Moore Foundation
Mercers' Company
The Monument Trust
The Rayne Foundation
Reuter Foundation
Sir John Cass's Foundation
Spitalfields Market Community Trust
Stanley Picker Foundation
The Wolfson Foundation
Worshipful Company of Butchers
Worshipful Company of Fanmakers
Worshipful Company of Grocers

Sponsors

AIB Bank
ANZ Grindlays Bank
Air India
Banker's Trust Company
Beck's
CDT Design Consultants
Foresight
Loot
Members of the Japan Merchant Bankers Association
Phoenix Electrical Company Ltd
Skidmore, Owings & Merrill Inc
Time Out
TSB Group plc
Unilever

Benefactors

Arthur Andersen & Co
David and Janice Blackburn
Cox & Kings Travel Ltd
Deutsche Bank AG, London Branch
Erco Lighting Ltd
London Stock Exchange
MoMart plc
Morgan Stanley International
Romulus Construction Ltd
Sedgwick Group plc

Donors

Brixton Estate plc
Ehrmann's Wine Shipping Ltd
Grand Metropolitan Estates
JP Morgan
Annely Juda
Sir Kit McMahon
Sir Robert and Lady Sainsbury
Troughton McAslan

Corporate Patrons

Ashurst Morris Crisp
Berwin Leighton
Botts and Company Ltd
Greycoat plc
Freshfields
Hanover Acceptances Ltd
The Members of Lloyd's & Lloyd's Brokers
Nomura Bank International plc
Save & Prosper
Sheppard Robson
Stanhope Properties plc

The Whitechapel Group

Thomas Ammann
James Bartos
Dorothy Berwin
Robert Brown
James and Clare Kirkman Trust
Stuart Lipton
London Weekend Television
George Louden
Morgan Grenfell & Co
Oliver Prenn
Mrs J. Ritblat
Philip Sales
Christina Smith
The Hon Mrs R. Waley-Cohen

American Friends of the Whitechapel Art Gallery Foundation

The Andy Warhol Foundation for the Visual Arts Inc
David McKee Gallery
Douglas S. Cramer Foundation
Horace W. Goldsmith Foundation
Peter L. Kellner
Stuart and Susan Lucas
Readers' Digest Association Inc
Edith Simpson
Susan Weingarten

Exhibition

Curator
Catherine Lampert

Coordination
Felicity Lunn
Rebecca Hurst

Transport
John S. Connor
Fentons
Masterpiece International
Möbeltransport
TTI
West Coast Keating

General Transport Coordination
Momart plc

Photography
Courtesy James Kirkman Ltd., London
Courtesy Marlborough Fine Art Ltd
Courtesy Saatchi Collection, London
Courtesy The Art Institute of Chicago
Courtesy The Cleveland Museum of Art
Courtesy The Museum of Modern Art, New York
Courtesy The Saint Louis Art Museum
Courtesy Thomas Ammann Fine Art AG
Courtesy Thomas Gibson Fine Art Ltd.
Prudence Cuming Associates Ltd., London
Lee Stalsworth
Dorothy Zeidman

Framing
Riccardo Giaccherini Fine Frames, London

Catalogue
Design: Derek Birdsall
Production: Martin Lee, Omnific Studios
Coordination: Felicity Lunn and Rebecca Hurst
Printing: Amilcare Pizzi S.p.A., Milan

Trade distribution outside the UK and EEC countries by:
Rizzoli International Publications, Inc.
300 Park Avenue South, New York, NY 10010
ISBN 0–8478–1775–X

Printed and bound in Italy

The Whitechapel Art Gallery is grateful to Her Majesty's Government for its help in agreeing to indemnify the exhibition under the terms of the National Heritage Act 1980 and to the Museums & Galleries Commission for its assistance in arranging this indemnity. In New York, an indemnity has been granted by the United States Government Federal Council on the Arts and the Humanities.